EDITOR'S LETTER

CELEBRATING RARE FOOD STORIES FOR SPRING AND SUMMER

Welcome to the first issue of FOOD STORIES; this season's edit celebrating rare food brands - how exciting to be saying that! We are a seasonal publication and our first issue is themed on spring and summer. The celebration of rhubarb inspired the gorgeous colour of our front and back covers. Don't miss the fabulous Sweet and Tart Rhubarb Yoghurt Ice Cream recipe inside the back cover - a winner for any spring/summer entertaining.

My company, The Rare Brand Market, celebrates independent brands and products that are genuinely RARE and which often have the most wonderful back stories. We think shopping should be totally pleasurable and believe there is an art to shopping wisely. With the publication of Food Stories, we were aware that discovering artisanally produced food can be hard work unless you happen to have a wonderful Farm Shop or Deli in your neighbourhood! Let Food Stories help you. At the end of each specialist product and recipe featured, there is a direct shopping link you can use via our website www.therarebrandmarket.co.uk one click and you can order our 'edit' direct to your door.

Cover:
Smoked Mackerel and
Rhubarb Salad from
www.shootingpeas.com
Scott James, founder of
Coaltown Coffee
www.coaltowncoffee.co.uk

WWW.THERAREBRANDMARKET.CO.UK

It is undeniable that there is a place for supermarket/big brand shopping in our lives. However, if we apprciated small production, artisanial food more we would be delighted with the transparency of our food source and bowled over by the supremely better taste of our food.

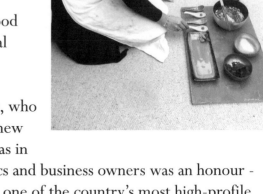

In this issue there are over 50 seasonal recipes, double the amount your average cookbook gives you. You will also be able to read brilliantly written articles about current global food trends. Food Stories really is this season's edit of rare food brands and topical news.

As the front cover says, Food Stories is powered by Great Taste, who have always set the benchmark so high in uncovering glorious new foods. Even before I was invited to join their judging panel I was in awe. To judge and taste alongside acclaimed food writers, critics and business owners was an honour - my most memorable day was sitting next to Charles Campion, one of the country's most high-profile food critics, and sniffing a lot of gin and beer!

Our Edit of the 2015 Great Taste winners have provided the content for the recipes.

James Golding, Chef Director of The Pig Hotel Group and fellow Great Taste Judge, has worked with me to ensure you have easy, innovative recipes for all your spring and summer eating. Action Against Hunger are our chosen charity partner. Do read about how we are supporting this worthy charity, further on in our introduction section.

Dictionary defined: "A foodie is a person who has an ardent or refined interest in food and alcoholic beverages. A foodie seeks new food experiences as a hobby rather than simply eating out of convenience or hunger." That is certainly me, a foodie through and through. I have always loved eating in season. My father nurtured a thriving fruit and vegetable garden growing up. So I was blessed with his organic bounty, made even more delicious by my mother's brilliant culinary skills. There is something so grounding about eating with the seasons. In today's chaotic world, anything that grounds us should be treasured.

Enjoy this labour of love ... please collect this publication to bring "seasonality" back to your kitchen and in turn please help us support smaller food brands who work so tirelessly to produce such quality driven, source transparent food and drink.

Emma Schwarz
Editor, Food Stories
Founder, Rare Brand Market

FOOD STORIES Contents

SUBSCRIBE AND SAVE 25%

SUBSCRIBE TO ALL THE SEASONS OF 2016 BY REGISTERING INTEREST ON OUR WEBSITE...

WWW.THERAREBRANDMARKET.CO.UK/FOODSTORIES

In Partnership with the Guild of Fine Food Ltd, Guild House, 23b Kingsmead Business Park, Shaftsbury Rd, Gillingham, SP8 5FB & Action Against Hunger, 1st Floor, Rear Premises, 161-163 Greenwich High Road, London, SE10 8JA. Charity No 1047501,

Contact enquries@therarebrandmarket.co.uk or call us on +44 (0)1243776682.

Copyright © 2016.

Printed in the United Kingdom by PPG Print www.ppgprint.co.uk . All rights reserved. Written production in whole or in part without written permission is strictly prohibited.

The title 'Food Stories' is in the process of registration by The Rare Brand Market Ltd as a trademark at the UK Trademark Office.

Recipe photography © 2016 Shooting Peas, www.shootingpeas.com

The Author, The Rare Brand Market Ltd, has asserted its rights under the Copyright, Designs and Patents Act 1988 to be identified as the author of this work.

ISBN 978-0-9926005-1-8

Advertising Enquires call +44 (0)1243776682 or email enquries@therarebrandmarket.co.uk

CONTRIBUTORS

Published in Great Britain in 2016 by The Rare Brand Market Ltd.

Registered Office: c/o Evans Weir, The Victoria, 25 St Pancras, PO19 7LT
Editor-in-chief & Creative Director: Emma Schwarz
Features Editor: Harriet Baxendale
Copy-Editor: Miriamme Rose
Cover Design: Sarah Ritchie www.sritchiedesign.com
Graphics: Alys Bryan
Advertising: Olivia Lukas
In-house Chef: James Golding
Writers: Rebecca Letty, Susannah Prain, James Hood, Sarah Tebb
Wine Writer: Helen McGinn
Beer Writer: Pete Brown
Mixologist: James Fowler
Food Photography: Dom & Helen Hoile www.shootingpeas.com
Health Food Researcher: Olivia Lukas www.nutrition-nutshell.com

GROW YOUR OWN FANTASTIC OYSTER MUSHROOMS IN 2 WEEKS!

Espresso Mushroom Company is a group of coffee drinking food lovers bringing you the ultimate in fresh, home-grown and sustainable product.

The kits are a great treat for you and your kids, and a perfect gift for green fingered foodies and garden-deprived city dwellers alike...

Introduction...

IN THIS SECTION WE INTRODUCE YOU TO THE ORGANISATIONS BEHIND FOOD STORIES...

Asparagus

ILLUSTRATIONS SUPPLIED BY WWW.SIVELLINK.DK

The team involved in the Recipe
Photoshoot.

From left to right:
John Farrand, Managing Director,
Guild of Fine Food, Organiser of
Great Taste
Helen Hoile, Co-founder of
www.shootingpeas.com
Dom Hoile, Co-founder of Shooting
Peas.
Emma Schwarz, Founder of
www.therarebrandmarket.co.uk and
Edit in Chief of Food Stories.
Harriet Baxendale, Features Editor of
Food Stories.
Tortie Farrand, Marketing director,
Guild of Fine Food, Organiser of Great
Taste.
James Golding, Chef Director at The
Pig Hotel Group.

**Photograph taken at
www.thepighotel.com**

Great Taste

I N 2014 THE RARE BRAND MARKET SENT THE GUILD OF FINE FOOD ITS SELF-PUBLISHED COOKBOOK. THE GUILD FELL IN LOVE WITH THE CONCEPT OF CELEBRATING SMALL PRODUCERS VIA RECIPES AND TELLING THE BACK STORIES OF EACH BRAND. TOGETHER THEY DECIDED TO HELP THE COOKBOOK BECOME A MAGAZINE. SO FOOD STORIES WAS BORN! READ HERE ABOUT THE GUILD'S BACK STORY...

In 1995, a small gathering of like-minded people got together and did something big to change the future of fine food – they started the Guild of Fine Food.

Little did they know that over 20 years later, there would be a food renaissance that has created a new wave of delis, farmers' markets, food co-operatives, farm shops, box schemes, food programmes and cookery schools.

Throughout all of these changes the Guild of Fine Food has been working tirelessly to encourage, promote and yes, often defend – fine food.

Great Taste is a major part of this drive. Recognisable by the little black and gold logo often seen on a jar, packet, bottle or box, Great Taste is organised each year by the Guild of Fine Food and, each year, more than 450 judges taste their way through everything from strawberry jam to stuffed olives, salt aged beef to espresso and sourdough to single variety cider.

The process is rigorous; judges have to confer and agree. That's why Great Taste is respected by fine food retailers and producers. It has been referred to as the Michelin Stars of the fine food world. This year, 10,000 products will be blind-tasted by Great Taste judges. By blind-tasting we mean no packaging, no idea of who made the product, no clue as to whether the jam was made by a well-established preserve business, or a small artisan producer making jam by hand with one bubbling pot. The only thing that carries weight with Great Taste judges is taste.

Yes, it does sound like a job made in heaven, so who are these judges? They are chosen from the world of food; chefs, food critics, food writers, restaurateurs, fine food retailers, bakers and more. Each judge brings a different skill to the table.

Every entry is equal and each judge tastes with one thing in mind, they are looking for outstanding food and drink and when they find it, they award the coveted Great Taste stars. While they taste, they are talking, commenting, identifying flavours and providing feedback which is all captured for the producer as this is a valuable part of the whole process.

Feedback, be it positive, complimentary or providing helpful suggestions for improvement, is a major part of Great Taste judging.

Judges work in teams and for a product to be given 3-stars, as many as 25 judges will have tasted and agreed that the food or drink was faultless.

Last year only 130 foods achieved the highest rating, 3-stars. 597 foods grabbed 2-stars and 2382 were awarded a 1-star. That means only 31% of entries were accredited – it's tough. All this sipping, nibbling, sniffing and cogitating culminates in eight Golden Fork winners and one Supreme Champion.

In 2015, the Great Taste Supreme Champion was butcher, James Whelan, for beef dripping made from suet from his grass-fed Irish Angus and Hereford cattle, "a pure distillation of bovine goodness", agreed the judges.

Next time you hit the shops, look out for those little Great Taste stickers on jars, bottle and packets – they are worth picking up and tasting for yourself!

www.greattasteawards.co.uk

ACTION AGAINST HUNGER

FOOD STORIES WANTED TO COMBINE THEIR PASSION FOR FOOD WITH AIDING A WORTHY CAUSE. CHOOSING A CHARITY WITH FOOD AT ITS CORE WAS A NO-BRAINER. IT SEEMED RIGHT TO RAISE MONEY AND AWARENESS ABOUT THOSE WHO ARE HUNGRY IN THE WORLD. ACTION AGAINST HUNGER UK ARE LEADERS IN THIS FIGHT AND ARE WORKING TOWARDS A GOAL TO END MALNUTRITION ACROSS THE GLOBE. FIND OUT HERE WHY THEIR CAUSE IS SO RELEVANT TODAY...

Food is a passion for many, and a need for all. At Action Against Hunger, we love opportunities to collaborate with people passionate about food, who understand its power to bring people together. The publication of Food Stories is a perfect example of unifying people with food. The Guild of Fine Foods and The Rare Brand Market are working with The Pig Group of hotels and a host of independent producers to create a unique publication celebrating the passion all the partners share in good food. The result is a unique recipe resource. Food Stories is a quarterly reflection of the food scene in the UK today, and whether your culinary aspirations are tasty toast toppers or something more ambitious, it is about releasing your kitchen potential.

Fulfilling potential is always at the forefront of our minds at Action Against Hunger. This year, we want to reach out and get people talking about how access to good nutrition is the best possible start a child can get in life.

Globally, 50 million children under the age of five are acutely malnourished. These children are not only hungry, but in the long term are much less likely to overcome life threatening disease, complete their education, or go on to live prosperous lives as adults. Something as basic as nutritious food in the first 1000 days of a child's life, has a profound impact on everything that follows.

As leaders in the fight against hunger, we are battling to ensure these children are getting the proper start in life. Action Against Hunger work in 46 countries, helping communities get access to adequate nutrition, clean water and better sanitation. We provide a strong voice to fight for them around the world.

By diagnosing and treating malnourished children in their communities, rather than in hospitals, we have made enormous progress in reaching increasing numbers of children. So now, more children are getting that vital healthy, nutritious start in life; more children will have the opportunity to reach their potential.

New global goals came into effect at the beginning of this year, resulting in an ambitious international agreement by all nations. The year 2030 has been set as the date to end hunger and malnutrition around the world. We want all children to live in a world without hunger - wouldn't that be an amazing ambition to be a part of?

All this progress wouldn't be possible without our supporters. We want to thank the brilliant team at Food Stories for their fantastic support and are delighted that a third of Food Stories profits will go towards our work to put an end to world hunger. This kind of fantastic generosity goes a long way to ensure that those who are passionate about food are giving the best possible help to those most in need.

www.actionagainsthunger.org.uk

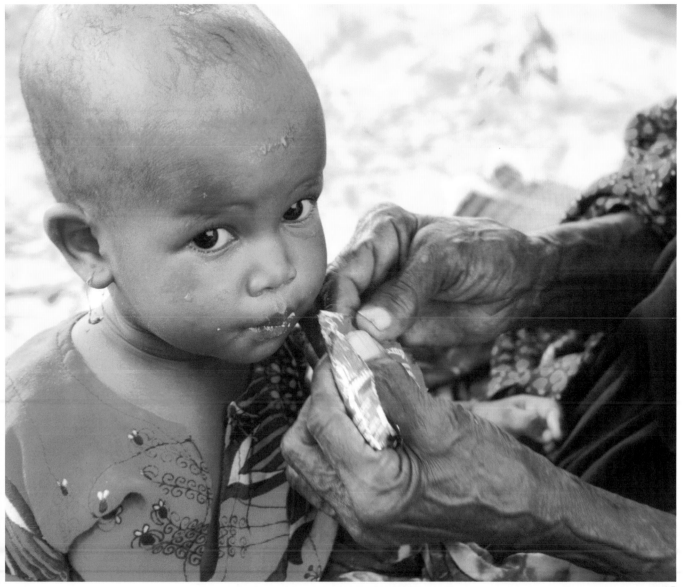

THE GOLDING RULE

JAMES GOLDING, GREAT TASTE AWARD JUDGE AND CHEF DIRECTOR AT THE PIG HOTEL GROUP IS ON LOAN TO FOOD STORIES. FOOD STORIES WANTED TO WORK WITH A RECIPE DEVELOPER AND CHEF WHO CARES ABOUT LOCAL FOOD AND SMALL PRODUCERS AS MUCH AS THEY DO. THE PIG HOTELS' WHOLE ETHOS CELEBRATES REGIONAL DIVERSITY AND JAMES WAS KEEN TO COOK WITH THE BEST INGREDIENTS FROM THE GREAT TASTE WINNERS.

After the gloom of the recession in the early 1990's, the emerging generation of chefs were ready to thrill us with exotic ingredients airfreighted in from the four corners of the world. A culinary trilogy - complex cookery, refrigerated ingredients flown hundreds of air miles and an insatiable thirst for food to dazzle. Over the next ten years there was an obsession with value, the rise of the BOGOF deal and people eating on the go - was everyone suddenly so hungry and so busy?

Sometimes its takes the most confidence to do the simplest things. James Golding, head of the kitchens at The Pig Group of hotels, was one of a handful of chefs with the chutzpah to change all that. In 2009, together with The Pig owner and founder, Robin Hutson, they gently kick started a revolution that is so simple in its evolution, it has the rest of us slapping our heads and wondering why we didn't think of it ourselves.

At the four Pig restaurants they have installed a radical food policy - the 25 mile menu. Genius. Eighty per cent of ingredients served at the restaurants have to be farmed, fished or foraged within 25 miles of The Pig or grown in the kitchen garden. The honey, the oysters, even the truffles - everything on the Pig's menu is local.

"When we open a new Pig, we spend six months visiting and talking to local suppliers of meat, fish, bread and cheese. It is exciting to discover the best an area has to offer and then work with these producers on a daily basis," says Golding.

It is all about the Kitchen Garden - the heartbeat of what they do. Guests who are doubting the true sustainability of the project, can walk around the garden and see the ingredients growing and being picked before it is prepared and served for lunch or supper. "I have been very lucky," smiles Golding, "I have had plenty of influences in my life who have shown me how wonderful food is often growing out the back door and how to get it on the menu as quickly as possible. A lot of chefs today still order their food in and away they go. But we want to do something different, so we try to educate the staff in the kitchens. It is not a spin cycle of briefly modish ingredients but how food goes from seed to plate. Simple." Hutson is in complete agreement and attributes The Pig's success to the million details needed to create excellence. "Quality, fresh products; an engaged team; great marketing; inspired surroundings," explains Hutson, "are just the start. Hotels have to understand that they need to become local destinations. They need to create food and beverage experiences that are relevant and part of the surrounding community, whether this be the business community, local residents, tourists or passing trade – they need to deliver emotion."

It is difficult to capture the menu, as who knows what the gardeners and fishermen will harvest today. There is no set routine and that is part of the experience. You either get it or you don't. Put your trust in those who know what they are doing in the kitchen. Yes, they work to a defined set of principles, but this does not limit their cooking. Rather it gives them a freedom to serve increasingly simple food which is a pleasure to have in front of you. Nostalgically forward thinking.

When it comes to The Pig and its pioneering chef, the accolades are as far flung as his meals are not. Pure happiness on a plate.

THE PIG

ROOMS &
KITCHEN GARDEN FOOD

www.thepighotel.com

Celebrity Edit...

WE ASKED THREE CELEBRITY CHEFS TO SHARE A SPRING OR SUMMER RECIPE FROM THIER LATEST BOOK AND SUGGEST A GREAT TASTE WINNING INGREDIENT.

Chard

Adam Handling

ADAM'S LATEST COOKBOOK 'SMILE OR GET OUT OF THE KITCHEN' IS OUT NOW, PUBLISHED BY MEZE PUBLISHING.

At only 27 and with many awards and accolades already under his belt, Chef Adam Handling is inspiringly ambitious and a rapidly rising talent. A highly accomplished chef with a central London restaurant, Adam Handling at Caxton, Adam's dishes are sourced with seasonal ingredients of the highest quality. His current 'tastes and textures' menu is inspired by his own travels, adventures and memories. With a love of Asian flavours and cooking techniques - particularly Japanese - his beautifully presented dishes showcase his creativity with flavour combinations and exceptional technical skill.

The youngest person to be tipped by the Caterer Magazine as one of the '30 under 30 to watch' in the 2013 Acorn Awards, Adam has since been awarded the British Culinary Federation's Chef of the Year 2014, Newcomer Restaurant of the Year in the Food and Travel Reader Awards 2015, as well as reaching the finals of National Chef of the Year 2016.

WWW.ADAMHANDLING.CO.UK

Smoked Halibut Spring Risotto

This smoked halibut risotto is not like traditional risotto laced in butter and Parmesan, but instead a lighter approach softened by the crème fraîche and underlying smoked fish tones.

For the risotto base

250g arborio rice
6 shallots, finely diced
3 garlic cloves, puréed
100ml white wine
300ml fish stock
In a heavy-based saucepan melt the butter and add the finely diced shallots and garlic.
Cook for 20 minutes on a low heat until soft and translucent.
Pour in the arborio rice and stir, allow the rice to snap which means the starch is releasing.
Add the white wine and reduce.
Add the stock, ladle by ladle, cooking slowly, until the rice is al dente.

To garnish

Chopped chives
Crème fraîche
Fresh spring peas
Parmesan
Picked chervil
Salt and pepper to season
Warm the risotto in a saucepan.
Finish with crème fraîche, chives, peas and Parmesan.

The Halibut

200g of Gigha smoked halibut www.gighahalibut.co.uk
Simply add in the slices smoked halibut and allow the heat of the risotto to gently warm the fish (this only needs to be brief and is simply to allow the fish to warm slightly and not to cook.)
Season to taste and garnish with fresh chervil or other herbs of your choosing.

Madeleine Shaw

MADELEINE'S LATEST COOKBOOK 'READY, STEADY GLOW' IS OUT NOW, PUBLISHED BY ORION.

Madeleine is a qualified nutritional health coach, yoga instructor, Sunday Times bestselling cookery writer and creator of the Glow Guides app, the first holistic 'transformational programme'.

Her philosophy is simple: ditch the junk and eat your way to a healthy lifestyle that is both sustainable and delicious. She cooks with wholefoods, meat, fish and plenty of flavour - and is a strong advocate for focusing on the good stuff, rather than beating yourself up about the bad.

Madeleine has her own range of healthy food in the Harrods Food Hall, is the host of Endemol's new food channel 'Wild Dish', and is Origins' official Glow Girl for 2016. Her Glow Guides app is available to download in the App Store.

WWW.MADELEINESHAW.COM

Ginger Beef Kebabs with Yogurt and Salad

On the move or in a hurry? This is the perfect answer to such situations. You have wonderful immunity boosters in the garlic and ginger, and the coconut oil doesn't denature the goodness of the other ingredients, due to its high smoking point.

Serves 2

1 tbsp freshly grated ginger

1 tbsp gluten-free tamari, soy sauce or Liquid Aminos

1 tbsp Wild Oak Honey www.eulogiausa.com

2 cloves garlic, crushed

1 tbsp coconut oil, melted

250g beef (sirloin or rump steak), cut into 2.5cm cubes

100g natural yoghurt

3 tbsp olive oil

25g watercress

25g rocket

salt and pepper

In a bowl combine the ginger, tamari, Liquid Aminos or soy sauce, honey, 1 garlic clove and melted coconut oil, then throw the beef in. Leave this for at least 2 hours and up to 12 hours in the fridge if you can; however it will still taste great if you don't have that long.

Thread the beef on to 4 skewers. (If using wooden or bamboo skewers, soak them in water first.) Heat a griddle pan to a medium to high heat and cook the kebabs for 5 minutes, rotating every minute so they cook evenly.

Mix the yoghurt with the remaining crushed garlic, the olive oil and a grind of salt and pepper. Serve the dressing on the side, or drizzled over the watercress, rocket and kebabs.

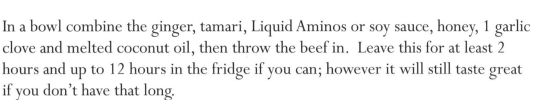

James Golding

JAMES' LATEST COOKBOOK 'WILDCOOK,' WRITTEN WITH GARRY EVELEIGH, IS OUT NOW, PUBLISHED BY ZSAZSEVA PUBLISHING.

James' career has spanned over 20 years. His career started at The Savoy in London where he gained a firm grasp of classical French cooking. He then moved to Caprice Holdings, where he worked mainly at Le Caprice under Mark Hix, and later Elliot Ketley. James also worked in Le Caprice's other venues; J Sheekey and The Ivy. Elliot Ketley then hired James as Head Chef of the 6th floor restaurant at Soho House, New York. After becoming a father James moved back to England and was Head Chef at the acclaimed Sandbanks restaurant Harbour Heights, but was soon hired by hotel guru Robin Huston to head up the chef team at The Pig Hotel Group, which was formed in 2009.

James is currently very busy with the launch of the latest Pig Hotel which opens this summer in Devon. The Pig Hotel is winning countless top awards including recently 'Top 100 Restaurants' for the 3rd year and a 'Catey' (the Oscar equivalent for the hotel industry).

WWW.THEPIGHOTEL.COM

A Pinch Of Salt Karma Ham Salad With Pickled Winter Chanterelle

Serves 4 as a starter

1kg wild chanterelles
250ml water
250ml white wine vinegar
4 garlic cloves
2 sprigs of thyme
3 cloves
5 juniper berries (dried are fine)
1 tsp black peppercorns
½ tsp salt
2 bay leaves
500ml olive oil, approximately
a few peppercorns, bay leaves & fresh thyme for garnish
150g rocket, stemmed & washed
2 heads of chicory, separated into leaves
10 slices of A Pinch of Salt air dried Karma Ham www.apinchofsaltcuring.co.uk cut into thin strips, or equivalent
10 semi-dried tomatoes cut into thin strips
¼ red onion, very finely shaved
a few basil leaves, roughly torn
a handful of pine nuts, toasted
50g pecorino shavings

Dressing:

3 tbsp extra virgin olive oil
1 tbsp red wine vinegar
1 pinch of ground nutmeg
salt & pepper
Italian pickled wild mushrooms
Yield: 2 x 500ml jars

Carefully clean the mushrooms with a dry cloth making sure all detritus is removed. In a saucepan, combine the water, vinegar, garlic, thyme, cloves, berries, peppercorns, salt and bay leaves, bring to the boil and add the mushrooms. With a spoon, immerse the mushrooms in the marinade.

"My grandmother was Italian and my first memory of pickled mushrooms... the pan before she could get them into the jars. I still love them. Chantere... they dry out so this is the perfect way to preserve them to have on hand t...

WWW.APINCHOFSALTCURING.CO.UK
A PINCH OF SALT
A British Curing Company
01425 611278

Cook for 3 minutes on high heat then reduce the heat and simmer for 10 minutes until the mushrooms are tender. Drain the mushrooms, allow to cool and then divide into sterilised jars. Add a few peppercorns, bay leaf and sprigs of thyme and fill the jars with olive oil making sure the mushrooms are completely covered. Seal and marinate in the refrigerator for 15 days before serving.

In a salad bowl place the rocket, chicory, onion, Karma Ham, tomatoes, basil, half the pine nuts and pecorino. Mix together the oil, vinegar, nutmeg, salt and pepper. Toss together with the salad ingredients. Scatter with the remaining pine nuts and pecorino and top generously with the pickled mushrooms.

Food Stories Profiles...

IN THIS SECTION FOOD STORIES PROFILES YOUTH, TECHNOLOGY, SUSTAINABILITY AND AN INSPIRATIONAL FOUNDER IN THE FOOD INDUSTRY.

Strawberries

YOUTH IN DA KITCHEN

FOOD STORIES PROFILES A YOUNG, RISING FOOD STAR EACH ISSUE, 18 YEAR OLD AMY-BETH ELLICE IS BRITAIN'S YOUNGEST FEMALE PUBLISHED COOKERY AUTHOR, WITH HER DEBUT BOOK 'AMY'S BAKING YEAR' PUBLISHED WHEN AMY WAS JUST 16.

www.amybethellice.com
Twitter @amybethellice
Instagram @amybethellicebakes

WHITE CHOCOLATE, RASPBERRY & ROSE PETAL CAKE

Preheat the oven to 180°C/fan 160°C/350°F/gas mark 4. Grease 2 x 20cm (8 inch) cake tins and line the bases with baking parchment.

For the cake:
350g (12oz) butter, plus a little more for greasing tins
350g (12oz) caster sugar
350g (12oz) self-raising flour
6 eggs
2 tsp vanilla extract
2 tsp rosewater

For the rose syrup:
110g (4oz) caster sugar
60ml (2fl.oz) water
1 tsp rosewater

For the white chocolate and rose buttercream filling:
110g (4oz) butter
225g (8oz) icing sugar
150g (5oz) white chocolate
1–2 tbsp milk
1 tbsp rose syrup
1 tsp vanilla extract

For the raspberry glacé icing:
110g (4oz) raspberries
275g (10oz) icing sugar

For the filling:
150g (5oz) raspberries

To decorate:
crystallised rose petals
crystallised rose fragments

Preheat the oven to 180°C/fan 160°C/350°F/gas mark 4. Grease 2 x 20cm (8 inch) cake tins and line the bases with baking parchment. To do this, draw around the base of the cake tins and cut out.

Put the butter, caster sugar, eggs, rosewater and vanilla extract into the bowl of a free-standing electric mixer (or you can use a handheld electric whisk and mixing bowl). Then sift in the flour, lifting the sieve quite high to incorporate air, and beat for 1–2 minutes until light and creamy. Divide the mixture between the two cake tins, smoothing the surface of the cake mixture with a spatula or the back of a spoon.

Bake for 45 minutes or until well risen and a skewer inserted into the middle of the cakes comes out clean. Leave to cool in the tins for 10 minutes. Turn out onto a wire rack, peel off the baking parchment and leave to cool completely.

To make the rose syrup, put the sugar in a pan with 60ml (2fl.oz) water and heat until the sugar has dissolved. Turn up the heat and let it bubble for 1–2 minutes, then remove from the heat. Add the rosewater (be careful as the syrup will be very hot). Spoon half the syrup over the cakes and set aside.

Melt the white chocolate in a bowl over a pan of gently simmering water, making sure the water is not touching the bottom of the bowl. Stir the mixture every now and then until all of the chocolate has melted. Leave the melted chocolate to cool until needed.

Meanwhile, prepare the white chocolate and rose buttercream. Beat the butter until soft and creamy. Sift the icing sugar and gradually add with the milk to the creamed butter mixing on a low speed. When fully incorporated add 2 tbsp of the syrup, the rosewater, the vanilla extract and the cooled chocolate and beat for 3–5 minutes on a higher speed until soft and fluffy.

Add 1 tbsp of the syrup to the raspberries and crush them with a fork. Put the raspberries through a sieve into a bowl and discard the seeds. Sift in the icing sugar and mix to a smooth icing.

To assemble, place one cake, flat-side up, on a plate or cake stand, and top with the white chocolate and rose buttercream and then arrange the raspberries on top. Sandwich the second cake on top. Pour and smooth the raspberry glacé icing over the top, letting it drizzle down the sides. To decorate, I used my handmade crystallised rose petals and crystallised rose fragments.

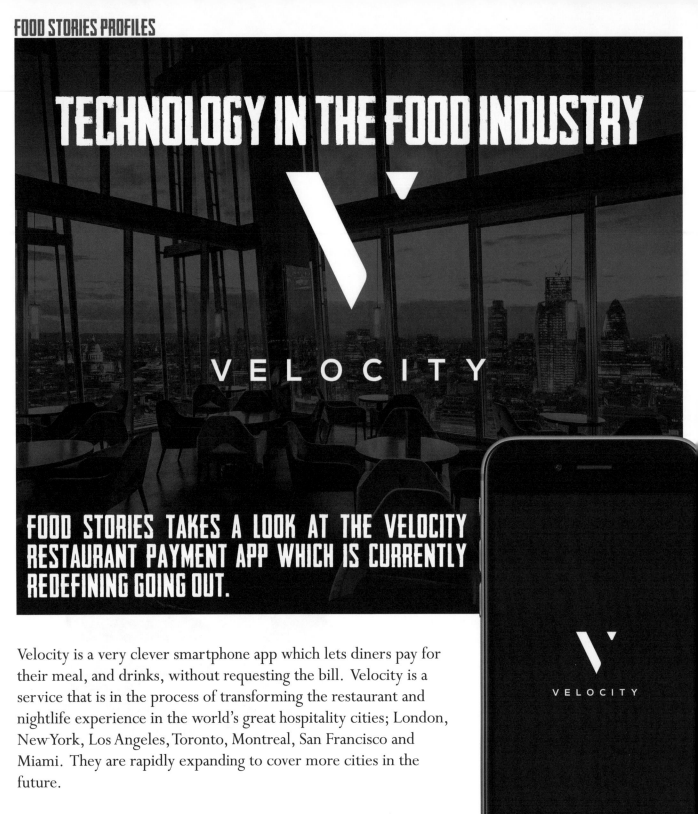

TECHNOLOGY IN THE FOOD INDUSTRY

VELOCITY

FOOD STORIES TAKES A LOOK AT THE VELOCITY RESTAURANT PAYMENT APP WHICH IS CURRENTLY REDEFINING GOING OUT.

Velocity is a very clever smartphone app which lets diners pay for their meal, and drinks, without requesting the bill. Velocity is a service that is in the process of transforming the restaurant and nightlife experience in the world's great hospitality cities; London, New York, Los Angeles, Toronto, Montreal, San Francisco and Miami. They are rapidly expanding to cover more cities in the future.

Through the Velocity app you can make reservations, read exclusive restaurant reviews and even book a taxi to your chosen destination.

To download the Velocity app please visit www.velocityapp.com

FOOD AND SUSTAINABILITY

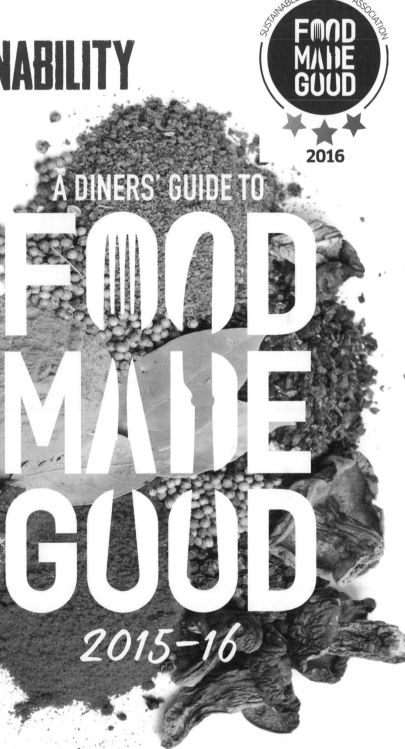

The British have fallen head over heels in love with eating out and now enjoy an incredible 8 billion meals a year that they haven't had to cook.

However, if it drives you mad when restaurants serve fish that's about to disappear from the oceans, won't explain where the tips are going, or refuse to provide a doggy bag when your eyes prove bigger than your tummy, fear not, help is at hand.

For those too shy to challenge the waiter, there's a new way of checking out the credentials of more than 5,000 restaurants, cafés, pubs and hotels from the South Coast of England, to Shetland. Food Made Good provides a platform for everyone who's passionate about their food and cares about where it's from.

Most importantly food lovers can look for the Food Made Good stars awarded to restaurants that have been assessed across everything they do, by the Sustainable Restaurant Association (SRA) - known as the Michelin Stars of sustainability; they also produce a Diners' Guide which is worth checking out.

So, next time you're planning to indulge your passion for dining out, don't check your principles in at the cloakroom, check out Food Made Good.

www.foodmadegood.org

A DINERS' GUIDE TO FOOD MADE GOOD 2015-16

Packed full with recipes, events and a directory of sustainable restaurants

SUSTAINABLE RESTAURANT ASSOCIATION

FOOD MADE GOOD

2016

RUBIES IN THE RUBBLE FOUNDER

Jenny Costa talks to Rebecca Letty

THE FOUNDER OF RUBIES IN THE RUBBLE, STARTED HER BUSINESS MORE THAN FIVE YEARS AGO PICKING THROUGH THE WASTE BINS OF COVENT GARDEN MARKET, HER COMPANY HAS BEEN CHOSEN AS ONE OF 2016'S EVERLINE FUTURE 50.

Who is your food hero?
Jo Wright, a wonderful outlook, a true heart for helping others and incredibly inspiring and creative cooking with the ingredients they have. I love Jo's 'Food waste Fridays'!
www.simplybeingmum.com

What is your favourite road trip food?
If I've a co-pilot, houmous, olives, crackers - a load of tapas style snacking! I love picnic road trips - my sister and I had a pretty spectacular yogurt and granola spill across the dashboard on our last outing.

What is your guilty food pleasure?
Toffee! The best is old-fashioned, chewy toffee that comes in slabs and you almost need a hammer to break.

What is your most evocative childhood food memory?
Heading out to catch mackerel in our old rowing boat on summer holidays at home in Scotland. Making a fire on the beach and cooking it up for lunch.

Can you recommend a different food combination to try?
Watermelon and feta cheese. Really good.

RUBIES
IN THE RUBBLE

Food Stories Journalism...

FOOD STORIES HAS WRITTEN 12 ARTICLES ABOUT CURRENT GLOBAL FOOD SUBJECTS.

Artichoke

ILLUSTRATIONS SUPPLIED BY WWW.SIVELLINK.DK

A Jar of Magic

Written by Susannah Prain

GONE ARE THE DAYS WHEN THERE WERE LIMITS TO WHAT AND HOW MANY FLAVOURS COULD BE CONTAINED WITHIN A LITTLE JAR....FOOD STORIES CELEBRATE THE ALCHEMY AND CREATION OF LITTLE POTS OF WONDER.

The art of preserving food has acted as a necessity for certain cultures for thousands of years and was a vital means of ensuring people could eat healthily through the leaner months of the year. Jarred food, synonymous with staples such as mayonnaise, sauces and jam has become considerably more interesting over recent years. Vicky Smith is the Jamsmith. What she can't harvest from the orchard or hedgerows, she sources from local farmers' markets or growers' small-holdings and proceeds to create jams, jellies and fruit butters. Her approach is innovative, often pairing fruit with unorthodox flavours such as fennel blossom, basil and liquorice, the latter chosen to compliment the damsons from her orchard. Essentially a jam club, the concept is compelling for a clientele that enjoy seasonal, freshly prepared, small batch conserves with an original angle.

When Maureen Suan Neo decided to retire from her restaurant business Singapura, in the City of London several years ago, customers were reluctant to let her go. "How else

can we eat your food?" they asked me. "I had been making large batches of sauce for the restaurant, so it occurred to me that this was a way of continuing to share my cooking." The decision led to the bottling of signature sauces, steeped in heritage and flavoured with a myriad of Asian spices and herbs. Suan Neo supplies her Nonya's Secrets range of sauces, 'mixes' and oils to markets, delis, butchers and farm shops.

For Vicky Smith and Maureen Suan Neo, packing flavour and freshness into a jar is the result of a creative and nostaligic personal process.

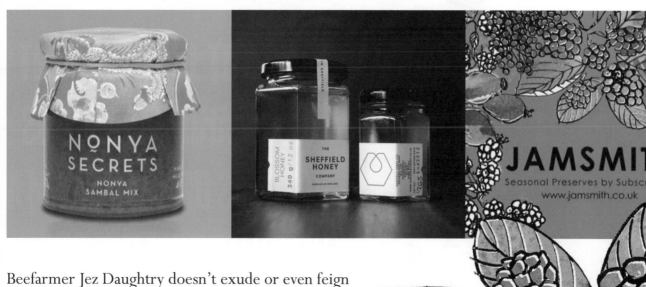

Beefarmer Jez Daughtry doesn't exude or even feign romance when he recalls his route to creating The Sheffield Honey Company. "I'd been made redundant from my job in IT; I was very disillusioned. I somehow got it into my head that I would produce a honey brand." Daughtry's initial plan was simple, create the brand, establish the colonies, harvest the product and sell it in the form of honey and beeswax candles. Starting with twenty hives in 2010, he now has approximately 400 hives across Sheffield extending into the Peak District and produces over 20 distinct honey products. Most of the colonies are situated in urban spaces including rooftops, gardens and parks and migrate with the help of boxed transportation to the heather moors and borage areas during the flowering season. Honey is one of nature's greatest foods, replete with minerals, enzymes and vitamins, a magic compound that once sealed will keep indefinitely. On the face of it, the plan was simple but through his progressive approach and an ability to diversify and share his knowledge, Daughtry may have inadvertently started a revolution in beekeeping. Keen to encourage more beekeepers, he runs workshops through his Urban Beekeeping Experience. Daughtry, like Vicky Smith and Maureen San Neo are not just preserving these delightful foods, they are preserving a way of life.

www.nonyasecrets.com
www.jamsmith.co.uk
www.sheffield-honey.co.uk

1st page: Pear illustrated by Kate Parkington. Maureen Suan Neo founder Nonya Secrets. This page, left to right: Sambal by Nonya Secrets. The Sheffield Company Honey. Jam by Vicky Smith founder Jamsmith. Blackberry illustrated by Kate Parkington.
Next page: Jez Daughtry founder The Sheffield Honey Company.

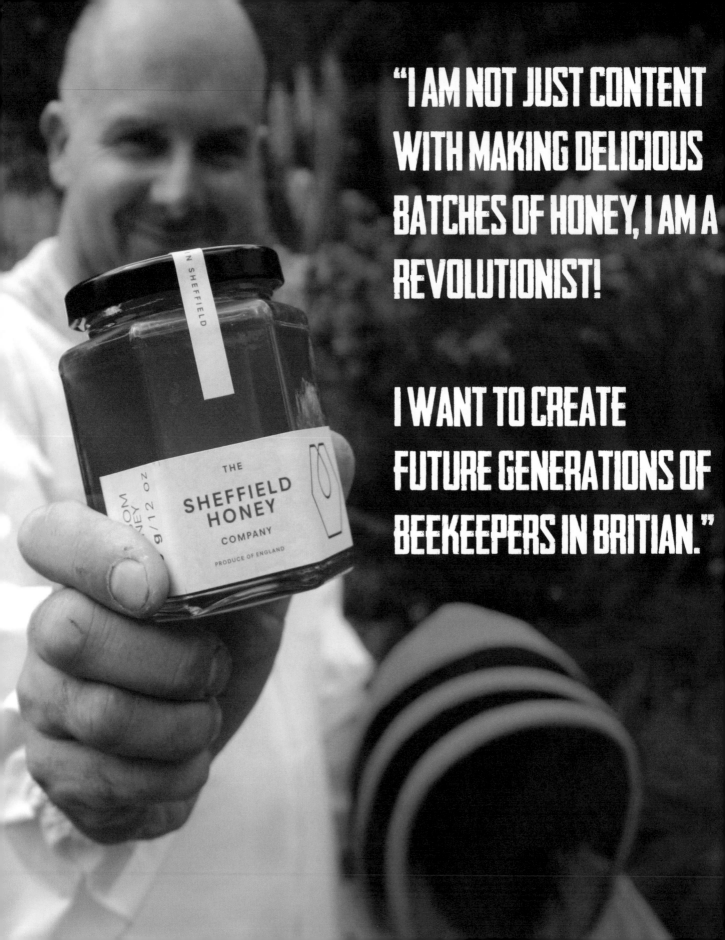

"I AM NOT JUST CONTENT WITH MAKING DELICIOUS BATCHES OF HONEY, I AM A REVOLUTIONIST!

I WANT TO CREATE FUTURE GENERATIONS OF BEEKEEPERS IN BRITIAN."

Food Keeping Communities Strong

Written by James Hood

FOOD STORIES TALKS TO THE OWNERS OF TWO BUSINESS THAT ARE BREATHING LIFE BACK INTO OTHERWISE FORGOTTEN WELSH TOWNS AND DISCOVERS THAT WITH A PINCH OF INGENUITY, AND COFFEE, YOU CAN REVIVE AN ENTIRE COMMUNITY.

It's fair to say that the landscape of 'industry' in the UK has seen some pretty significant changes over the last couple of decades. The decline of coal mining and steel manufacturing meant a major shift in employment in Wales and the North of England. Combine that with more recent trends towards digital services, and the result is a country that makes less and runs the risk of isolating rural communities from the big cities. But if there's one thing that is sure to bring people together in good times and in bad, it's a cup of coffee. So it's rather apt that a former mining town in Wales is in the process of being revived by a company manufacturing and serving the so-called 'black gold.'

COALTOWN
COFFEE ROASTERS

Ammanford in South Wales, has a population of just 5,500 people. After the closure of the town's colliery in 2003, Ammanford suffered from unemployment and low morale. Cue Coaltown Coffee, a company that has a simple purpose: to breathe life into the community again and give it a reason to shine. The people behind the business have decided coffee can save the town, boosting the locals' sense of pride and community.

Owner Scott James, who has lived in the town for his entire life, told Food Stories Magazine "My great grandfather moved to Ammanford in 1901 and worked in the mines. My family has been here ever since. While there was a mining industry, the town had a great vibe – a thriving community of people, many of whom had career prospects connected to the colliery. But once it closed the town seemed to lose its spirit. When I started Coaltown Coffee, I had a vision the business could inject some life back into the area, give us all something to be proud of and give school leavers who wanted to stay in the town some prospects for work."

If you're wondering why Scott chose coffee, it's because it runs in the family. His parents, with whom he runs Coaltown Coffee, own a café in the town and are credited with bringing the area its first ever espresso machine. Now, together they run the coffee shop, which happens to have played a large part in the introduction of Coaltown Coffee. "When my parents opened the shop, it went crazy. People loved it and it really

"I JUST WANT TO GIVE THE PEOPLE HERE SOMETHING TO BE PROUD OF, TO PUT US BACK ON THE MAP."

lifted the area. So when I left school I decided to continue working in the business. My dad and I built a roaster to produce our own coffee, and the rest is history! Our coffee is now sold around the country, we're even in Selfridges, which is great news for the town. I just want to give the people here something to be proud of, to put us back on the map."

Coaltown Coffee plans to open a new building and roastery within six months, for which they will be hiring local employees and further improving the town's economy.

In another Welsh town, a similar story has unfolded after the revival of a derelict flour mill. In the words of the mill's manager, Liz Rose, the small town of Talgarth had become quiet and ghost-like following the closure of a nearby hospital in the 1990s where many people worked. There was not much going on in Talgarth until the owner of the original flour mill bequeathed the land to his nephew who decided to revive the old building back to its former glory. It re-opened in 2011 operating as a working mill where visitors can take a tour, and then stop at the café and bakery where flour, cakes, bread and pizzas are sold. Most importantly it has become a hub for the community as well as a tourist destination. "Talgarth used to be the poor relation to other places in the region, like Brecon. There was no reason to come. People just drove through or straight past us," Liz added. "Now they travel just to see the town and the mill."

Both Coaltown Coffee and Talgarth Mill are examples of how lives can be changed and communities brought together with a little thought, a lot of hard work and a sense of pride in one's heritage.

www.coaltowncoffee.co.uk
www.talgarthmill.com

1st page: Coaltown Coffee.
2nd page: 'Coffee' photography by Finn Beales.
This page: Flour bags at the Felin Talgarth Mill.

Wasteland Food

Written by Sarah Tebb

WASTE NOT WANT NOT - AS THE OLD SAYING GOES - THESE WORDS COULD NOT BE MORE RELEVANT TODAY. WE NEED TO LISTEN AND LEARN FROM THOSE LEADING THE WAY IN TRYING TO REDUCE OUR MASSIVE AMOUNTS OF WASTE.

The Western World produces up to 300 per cent more food than we actually need, yet over one billion people are suffering from malnutrition, something really doesn't add up. The UK alone is producing over 7 billion tonnes of food waste, this is not only costing us money but the environmental impact is unbelievably destructive. Luckily, there are some bright souls out there - champions in this field who are leading a serious, attitude revolution - one tomato tonne at a time.

One said champion is Jenny Dawson, founder of Rubies in the Rubble. Her company was born from the sheer shock of our national wastage stats. With her moral compass leading the way, Jenny is taking all those leftovers and making the most delicious chutneys and jams in the 'nicest possible way.' As well as being able to show how it is done, Rubies in the Rubble has given Jenny a platform on which to address the bigger issues of food sustainability, not only nationally but globally. Sourced only from surplus, her ingredients have to 'pass a taste test, not a beauty contest.' It really does make you question those perfectly shaped fruit and veg sitting pretty along the aisles of most supermarkets. Does a tomato really need to be perfectly cylindrical when it's about to be chopped up? Jenny has shown us, it really, really doesn't matter. Regardless of shape or size or how wonderfully wonky a vegetable is you can use it to create beautiful food in the end.

RUBIES
IN THE RUBBLE

And speaking of beautiful, Silo in Brighton are doing a brilliantly creative job in their restaurant. Their focus is all about respect and innovation. Their plates are made using solidified plastic bags and they share Bertha, an anaerobic digester turning waste into energy, with the community. They are going for zero waste and nailing it. Beer is brewed in the basement and served in old jam jars. It isn't about being trendy, it's about being realistic and understanding they have saved not only on physical waste but also energy. The energy that would have been wasted in recycling these objects. They are thinking outside the overly packaged box and are spelling out the bigger problem. They've taken zero waste as seriously as anyone can. As I tuck into my undeniably delicious breakfast; sourdough toast with silo baked beans and slow cooked egg, I understand their mentality in keeping the integrity of the ingredients intact and feeling invested in their cause. And I hope it spreads and innovates the food industry as we know it. Yes that might be dreaming big but these guys aren't here to move mountains, they're about reducing the size of our food wastage ones.

1st page: Jenny Dawson and Alicia Lawson, Rubies in the Rubble
2nd page: Jenny Dawson with her produce, Rubies in the Rubble
Previous page: Silo, 39 Upper Gardner St, Brighton, BN1 4AN
This page: The 'Love Food Hate Waste' food truck.

Thanks to Love Food Hate Waste, which was launched in 2007 with the aim of reducing the amount of food waste from all over the UK, the consumer can now follow guidelines and food plans learning day by day how to reduce the waste in their homes. Their website is informative, clear and easy to follow, making it so simple to change day to day practises, not only helping the environment but saving money which has to be a huge incentive on the daily shop. At least 7 million tonnes of food and drink are thrown from homes every 12 months which is costing nearly £13 billion a year, the campaign is aimed to educate by working with different organizations teaching how to waste less food. Their latest campaign is aimed at encouraging people to use their leftovers instead of just throwing them away. 'Meaty issues' was launched by Adam Henson on 25th February, and highlights top tips and easy to follow guidlines on how to waste less meat.

www.rubiesintherubble.com
www.silobrighton.com
www.lovefoodhatewaste.com

LOVE
FOOD
hate waste

Sydney
Food Scene Rocks

Written by Sarah Tebb

SYDNEY. THAT IS THE DESTINATION. AND MY OH MY IF YOU LIKE FOOD EVEN JUST A LITTLE BIT - THEN YOU'RE ABOUT TO WRACK UP A LOT OF AIR MILES. FROM THE BEARDED BAKERS TO A VIRAL JEWISH COOKING CLUB AND THE NEW BOROUGH MARKET, THERE REALLY IS SOMETHING GOING ON DOWN UNDER.

When three brothers decided they were going to take their mother's recipe and mix it with a little art, music and a shipping container, little did they know their pop-up bakery would have a dessert dance party on their hands. Knafeh is traditionally a heavy dish that is a meal in itself but these boys have made theirs lighter and creamier as well as taking it on the road. Everything about Knafeh is humble and the bakers, equipment and ingredients, reflects just that. Knafeh is street food taking the cultural experience to another level. The energy from their pop-up bakery, in a container, is festival like. The sound system have speakers as big as you can get. There is no groundbreaking science to this dish or

their concept. It is a simple celebration of a simple dish that simply works. The brothers want to take their Jerusalem Street Food to new audiences and break down the formalities of eating dessert. Now with a borderline cult following, they have successfully done just that. They've turned up the music and the queues are growing but this only heightens this brilliantly joyous affair.

Every Monday morning since 2006, the Monday Morning Cooking Club has met to chop and stir, mince and roll, roast and bake, fry and boil. This Sydney Sisterhood have tasted, eaten, laughed and debated, argued and agreed. These ladies wanted to show the world their unusually strong, somewhat

obsessive, connection with food. They don't send flowers, they bake a cake. When someone is ill, chicken soup arrives before the doctor and when a new baby is born they definitely make sure no-one in the family goes hungry. It is, most certainly, all about the food. Two cookbooks later, the Monday Morning Cooking Club is doing rather well, but this is a not-for-profit group . The huge amounts of money raised benefits a wide selection of Australian charities. Ten years on and with a growing fan-base, Yotam Ottolenghi being one of them, it is time to start sharing this generous and heartwarming story as well as the recipes.

The 'new' Borough Market, I can see some eyes roll already, but our home grown foodie destination has got some serious rivalry. Carriageworks Farmers Market is a visually stunning epicentre for all Sydney food lovers. Just like Borough market is one of London's worst kept secrets, Carriageworks has a similar loyalty and growing acclaim thanks to Creative Director, Mike McEnearney. He has developed a five core product charter: origin; knowledge; sustainability; authenticity and excellence. Quality of the produce takes centre stage. The flavours, the colours, the variety and the enjoyment we can all get from fresh produce. The Farmers Market is trying to 'reacquaint' people with this idea of seasonality and using the produce offered up from the natural bounty of Australia. Carriageworks has become a mouth-watering visual representation of the Australian food scene today. All we can say is watch out Borough Market, the Aussies are coming.

www.knafeh.com.au
www.mondaymorningcookingclub.com.au
www.carriageworks.com.au

CARRIAGEWORKS

1st page: The Crew at Knafeh, photography by Georges Antoni.
2nd page clockwise from top left: Knafeh, photography by Simon Shasa. The Girls of the 'Monday Morning Cooking Club.'
This page: 1st cookbook by Monday Morning Cooking Club, available in the UK. A busy day at the Carriage Works Farmers Market.

Globalization of Food on a Micro Scale

Written by Susannah Prain

FOOD STORIES DELVES INTO THE GLOBAL CHANGES IMPACTING, NOT ONLY ON OUR DAY TO DAY FOOD TASTES, BUT THE DIVERSITY OF DIFFERENT FOOD CULTURES AVAILABLE.

Travel and culture are embedded in human nature. When we visit other countries for work or pleasure, we absorb the food culture and return a little more educated, often yearning to discover and seek out more. Migration is exponentially growing across the globe, mainly due to displacement of people from areas of conflict or dwindling social and natural resources. The UK has experienced immigration across the centuries, but never before matched by the current numbers and multitude of origins and diverse cultures blending with society. We have a truly enviable spectrum of restaurants and food stalls serving anything from souvlaki to sushi and borak to burritos. As a nation we have been slow to embrace global food. Until recently immigrants from countries such as China, Italy and India have often had to modify their dishes to fit in with our palates and expectations.

MAZI MAS

"THESE WOMEN ARE COOKING VERY PERSONAL FOOD WITH A STORY BEHIND EACH DISH...WE ARE FORGING A CONNECTION BETWEEN DIFFERENT CULTURES."

Indian restaurants in the UK (often run by Bangladeshis and Pakistanis) have predominantly served Punjabi dishes or invented new ones to lend appeal such as the balti and chicken tikka masala, once described by Robin Cook as "a true British national dish." Marks and Spencer's track trends in restaurants and cookbooks in order to develop ranges. Their latest 'The Taste Collection' range celebrates global and regional food from Morocco, Istanbul, and Vietnam to name but a few. As a result of cheaper air travel to more destinations the British are discovering culinary pockets for themselves, and celebrity chefs on their televisual travels are broadening our horizons further. Increased air travel has also been a factor in availability of ingredients. Wishing to create a Puglian dish rather than just a generic Italian one means we can source the correct ingredients from specialist shops, markets and even supermarkets. The gradual evolution of the British taste for global food is entering our daily repertoire and we are now embracing it fully rather than tentatively dipping a toe in. Over recent years immigrants have opened restaurants serving authentic food true to the regions they hail from. Even British restaurateurs and chefs inspired by their own adventures abroad have opened restaurants dedicated to the cuisine they have fallen for, such as Sam and Sam Clarks' Moro and Thomasina Miers' at Wahaca. Food seems to bridge cultures and bring them closer often with spectacular results. Mazi Mas, meaning "with us" in Greek is a roaming restaurant dedicated to employing migrant and refugee women, founded and run by Niki Kopcke, a social activist and former volunteer at the community food charity FoodCycle in London. "It was at FoodCycle that I met Roberta Siao from Brazil. She was locked into a cycle of long-term unemployment, like so many women who have taken time out of work to raise children. Her story resonated on a personal level with that of my godmother's, a migrant to New York. These women and others like them were the inspiration for Mazi Mas." The enterprise employs between five and six women at any one time, from a range of countries including Nicaragua, Ethiopia, Turkey, Peru, Nepal and Senegal. Kopcke explains, "The idea was to create a platform to offer women the opportunity to showcase their skills and leverage them in to sustainable livelihoods where they could go on to make independent decisions about their lives and their children's lives." The initiative aims to further women's qualifications and careers so that they can continue to work in the food industry. "We recognize the skills they already possess and help them develop and formalize them." Three years on, and a successful crowd funding campaign assured their temporary restaurant at Ovalhouse Theatre in London, whilst maintaining their pop-up restaurants at Le Coq in Islington and Sutton House in Hackney. Mazi Mas is now in residence at The Russet in Hackney serving a truly eclectic list of global home cooking including Roberta's Linguiça, a blend of spicy Brazilian sausage and charred onions, Zohreh's Iranian saffron chicken and Azeb's Ethiopian berbere lentils, potato and beetroot, with flatbread. Kopcke, a chef herself believes in the powerful relationship between stories and food, "These women are cooking very personal food with a story behind each dish. Through bringing themselves and their cooking to Mazi Mas they are able to find a place and a sense of belonging in society where they are valued and respected. We are forging a connection between different cultures."

www.mazimas.co.uk
Twitter @eatmazimas

1st page: Zohreh and Azeb busy at Mazimas, photography by Gercama.

2nd page: Nikandre Kopcke founder Mazimas, photography by Elena Manfredi.

Food Steeped in Tradition

Written by Susannah Prain

AS A COUNTRY WE THRIVE ON TRADITION AND CEREMONY, SO LET US CELEBRATE THOSE FOR WHOM HERITAGE PLAYS SUCH AN IMPORTANT ROLE.

WORLD'S ORIGINAL

DALEMAIN
MARMALADE AWARDS

The annual Marmalade Awards generate a great deal of excitement across the 'marmalade community' principally in Britain, where marmalade is woven into the tapestry of our food heritage, accompanying the nation's morning toast and featuring in literary tales of James Bond and Paddington Bear. "It's a niche competition, so utterly British," says Jane Hasell-McCosh, founder of the Marmalade Awards. The list of principal sponsors and patrons reads like a Who's Who of British institutions, The Worshipful Company of Fruiterers, the Women's Institute, The Guiding Association, Fortnum and Mason, Mackays and Paddington Bear of course. The British relationship with marmalade dates back centuries when it was originally a paste made from quince. The bitter citrus element entered the repertoire in 1600s and became the archetypal flavour that we associate with marmalade today. Dalemain Mansion in Cumbria, home to the Marmalade Awards and the Hasell-McCosh family has its own unique relationship with marmalade. A book of recipes has resided at the house for over 300 years, containing a recipe for 'Marmalade of Oranges' and 'Bishop's Marmalade' written by the hand of Mr Hasell-McCosh's ancestor, Elizabeth Rainbow. The Bishop's Marmalade made from quinces and lemons has been lovingly honoured and recreated by Mrs Hasell-McCosh, and is available to buy from the Dalemain shop. Over 2000 jars from around the world have been entered in this year's Marmalade Awards fourteen categories. To the discerning palates of the current judges, to name a few, baker Dan Lepard, food historian Ivan Day and Pam 'the jam' Clements, the entries will be judged on appearance, set, aroma and flavour. The overall winner will have their recipe produced and stocked by Fortnum and Mason, "the ultimate British grocer" adds Hasell-McCosh.

'Drop as Rain, Distil as Dew' is the heraldic motto of the Worshipful Company of Distillers, a City of London livery company that was established in 1638 to regulate and supervise the production of spirits and liquors. Today the company is largely involved in charitable causes and educational initiatives and less so with the regulation of the distilling trade. Gin is going through something of a renaissance in the UK with independent distillers springing up in small garages, old breweries, creating gin with increasingly bold botanical flavours as well as the essential juniper. The Gin Guild is a recently incorporated industry body for gin distillers, an inception sparked by the new generation of craft distillers. Members of the guild are required to take a solemn oath to promote quality in gin distilling, and invited to attend an inaugural black-tie ceremony and dinner at Mansion House in the City of London with the Guild's parent company the Worshipful Company of Distillers.

The Gin Guild's Director General Nicholas Cook says "Gin is typically British - consider Hogarth's engraving Gin Lane, the ubiquitous Gin and Tonic and sloe gin."

The Gin Guild

"THE INEVITABLE LIGHT OF HISTORY THAT WILL SHINE SO FAVOURABLY ON THIS PARTICULAR WINDOW OF TIME IN GIN'S HISTORY IS A GREAT ONE AND IT MAKES IT EVEN MORE OF A PLEASURE AND HONOUR TO HAVE BEEN A PART OF IT. EVERY CATEGORY 'HAS ITS DAY' (AS IT WERE) AND FOR GIN IT HAS HAD A NUMBER OF CRESTS IN ITS TUMULTUOUS JOURNEY – THERE'S NO DOUBT THAT IT'S RIDING ANOTHER ONE NOW."

Sipsmith Gin, Co-founder, Sam Galsworthy

Sipsmith, a member of the Gin Guild, is a spirit distilling collaboration between stalwarts of the drinks industry, Fairfax Hall, Sam Galsworthy, Jared Brown, and Prudence, the copper still that produces small batches of London Dry gin and Barley Vodka. They are one of only a handful of gin distilleries located within London's city limits; another is Thames Distillers makers of forty-five different gins including Bath Gin. Conceived at The Canary Gin Bar in a little cobbled side-street in Bath by "ginisseurs," Peter Meacock, Harald Bret and Tim Whelehan, the Bath Gin Company set out to create "something modern, fresh and moreish" using botanicals including wormwood, the key ingredient in Absinthe and kaffir lime leaf, a feature of the rums of Madagascar, Reunion and Martinique. Their label is certainly a modern take on some Bath history, depicting a winking Jane Austen who, as well as setting two of her novels in Bath, had also lived there for four years and is reputed to have had a fondness for gin. Preparations are currently underway beneath the Canary Bar to create a basement distillery where the Bath Gin Company can produce their gin on site. It will be the first of its kind in Bath since the heyday of gin in the 1700s.

The history of gin and marmalade correspondingly, is an evolution inspired by exotic flavours sourced from across the globe, created with British craftsmanship and a good dose of traditional British standard.

www.sipsmith.com
www.theginguild.com
www.thebathgincompany.co.uk
www.dalemainmarmaladeawards.co.uk

1st page: The Marmalade Awards and Festival. From left to right, Marmalade on show at Dalemain Mansion, Penrith. The Gin Guild celebrating the Gin Industry.
2nd page left to right: Dalemain and the Gin Guild logo. An evening at the Gin Guild
Previous page: Sam Galsworthy and Fairfax Hall, founders Sipsmith. Behind them is Jared Brown Master Distiller.
This page, clockwise from top left: The Bath Gin Co. Botanicals at Sipsmith.

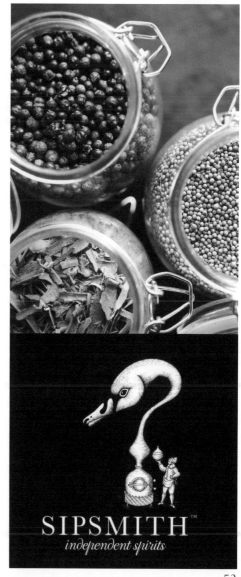

SIPSMITH™
independent spirits

A Tasty Legacy

Written by James Hood

WHILE MOST PEOPLE WOULD SHUDDER AT THE THOUGHT, WE DISCOVER THAT KEEPING A FOOD BUSINESS IN THE FAMILY CAN PROVE PRODUCTIVE, AND HELP YOU BUILD A LASTING LEGACY FOR GENERATIONS TO COME.

It's estimated that 60 per cent of businesses in the UK are family-owned. They create 9.4 million jobs in the country and contribute 25 per cent of the nation's GDP. So although the idea of working day in, day out with your own parents, children or siblings might fill you with dread, it's obviously a business model that works for some.

Warburtons, McVities and wine merchant Berry Bros and Rudd are just a few of the well-known family food or drink brands that have stood the test of time. And there are many you've probably never heard of that have also succeeded where others have failed, thanks to a family connection. One such business is Tims Dairy, which was started in central London in 1949 by the current owners' uncle, who came over to England from Cyprus. He was joined by their father to produce authentic Greek and Cypriot-style yogurts and desserts. As the business grew, the Chiltern Hills in Buckinghamshire became Tims Dairy's new home and their expertise has been able to flourish in the region ever since. Currently run by four brothers, Chris, Peter, Bides and Tony Timotheou, Tims Dairy has decades of family heritage in producing great tasting, award winning yogurts, all made with British milk and cream. The founding family ethos remains today - all natural ingredients, authentic recipes and great taste.

We all love a success story, particularly if it's an independent, but when you consider how many of us grumble at the thought of spending a couple of days with our families over Christmas, is it wise to start a business with any of them in the first place? For Richard Goring, the benefits include creating something lasting and a legacy that will continue his family's name and values. Together with his parents Harry and Pip, and his wife Kirsty, Richard runs Wiston Estate in Sussex. It has been in the family since 1743 and they recently planted a 16 acre vineyard. He told Food Stories Magazine: "For us, our business is a long-term investment. We run a vineyard, which took a lot of time and effort to set up and of course there's plenty of time dedicated to producing particular vintages of our sparkling wine. So you have to take a long-term view and adopt a strategy that will help you sustain the business in the future."

For others, the benefits of running a business with family lie in the variety of skills all members can bring to the table. Rupert Parsons is at the helm of Womersley, a producer of fruit and

WISTON
ESTATE
SOUTH DOWNS

"...YOU HAVE TO TAKE A LONG-TERM VIEW AND ADOPT A STRATEGY THAT WILL HELP YOU SUSTAIN THE BUSINESS IN THE FUTURE."

herb vinegars that operates from Chipping Norton, Oxfordshire. He told us that sharing knowledge and playing to each other's strengths has been crucial for the success of the company he runs along with his parents, Martin and Aline. "My father started Womersley in

1979 from my parents' home in Yorkshire, where they also ran a small craft shop. Dad created a raspberry vinegar that was great on your roast beef and Yorkshire puddings. And then he expanded, going on to produce a range of different fruit and herb-based products. When I joined the business in 2009, I refined the line, selecting eight vinegars and four jellies. I also rebranded the packaging to bring it up to date and make the products more modern, visually. I have business acumen but it is my dad who created the foundations to build upon, and that's something I acknowledge to this day. So identifying who is good at which role is important when you are working as a family", said Rupert.

When it comes to running any business, knowledge and expertise contribute to success. For family-run businesses, this can be easier to tap into than most, as there are often people with decades of experience on-hand. Rupert added: "My father was born at Nymans Gardens in Sussex, which is now a National Trust property. He was brought up learning about the plants and ingredients he would go on to use in his products. He

developed not only experience and knowledge, but a passion for the process. You can't buy that kind of contribution to a business. It's where having a second generation company gives you a real advantage." Even if you can find talented team members to hire for your own business, it can be hard to motivate others to share a passion for what you do. As Rupert puts it: "You could never employ someone to do the hours we do!"

Expertise on tap and the sharing of skills and knowledge are great for starting and keeping a business. But are there any drawbacks to running a company with family members? As Wiston Estate's Richard explains, planning the succession of a raural estate is not always straightforward. "In my family, there are six siblings including myself. So I think it takes a lot of consideration as to how you will pass on your business in that instance. Fortunately my father had always been clear that the estate would be past to one of us rather than be broken up, and that helped with expectation. My siblings have always been incredibly supportive of Kirsty and I but I don't think it's always as clear-cut. You have to have utter clarity of communication. From our own perspective, we have three sons, and although we hope one of them will want to take over the running of our business and estate, we would never force it upon them…"

Although there are clearly benefits to working together as a family, finding evidence that proves whether it's more or less fruitful is nearly impossible. After all, how can you judge the impact of external factors such as recession or internal elements like hiring exceptional staff members? How do you know if your business will be better if it's family-run? Richard added: "It's very hard to say without seeing it from the other side. I believe if it's something that comes from the heart. If you give it your all and you are motivated to see the business succeed then generally it will be a success. So to a certain extent you don't have to be a family run business to thrive - many businesses do very well that aren't family run. However, I couldn't do this without my mum and dad and vice versa. It works."

www.wistonestate.com
www.timsdairy.co.uk
www.womersleyfoods.com

2nd page: Richard Goring with son and father Harry Goring.

3rd page: Martin & Aline Parsons founders of Womersley, photography by Joan Russell. Rupert Parsons of Womersley Foods, photography by Jamie Harris.

This Page: The entire family at Wiston.

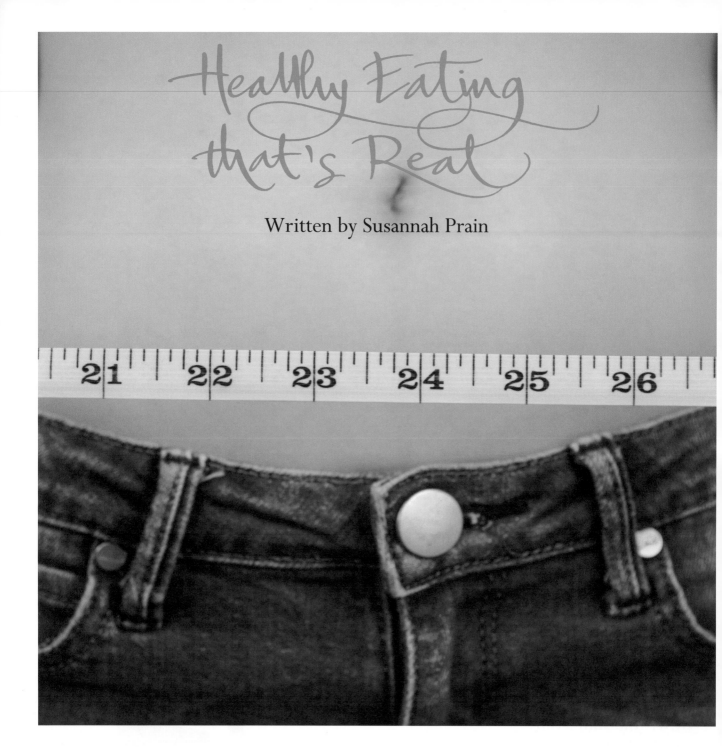

Healthy Eating that's Real

Written by Susannah Prain

FOOD STORIES SENSE THAT WE ARE ALL SICK OF HEARING ABOUT THE LATEST DIET OR FADS, COUPLED WITH ALL OF THE CONTRADICTIONS FROM HEALTH GURUS SUCH AS THE RECENT MIXED MESSAGES CONCERNING COCONUT OIL, OLIVE OIL AND BUTTER. IN THIS ARTICLE WE PROFILE A COMPANY RUN BY FASTIDIOUS GERMANS WHO TAKE THE PRINCIPLES OF WHAT WE EAT BACK TO THE BASICS.

How could something as simple as eating become so complicated? Distorted by professionals' and then fed back to us as indigestible jargon: good fats, bad fats, friendly and unfriendly bacteria! The modern-day plethora of diets claim to be backed up by scientific research and yet often contradict one another in what they hail as healthy. Consider, say, the abiding mixed messages over saturated fat; some dietitians consider it so evil, it is to be cast out of our diets as it will surely bring us down with heart disease triggered by high cholesterol. Others praise the ability of saturated fat to raise high-density lipoproteins, which are protective against heart disease, and others maintain that saturated fatty acids boost immunity and liver health. How can science be giving us such conflicting information?

We acknowledge that the foundation of food is scientific but surely through the millennia our ancestors have helpfully proven which foods sustain and nourish us and which are best avoided. If we let common sense prevail, we should be eating real food that grows and moves and avoid processed and artificial fodder.

Nutritionist, Dominique Ludwig of Nutrition Works says we need to get back to basics. She is a practitioner of Metabolic Balance™, a weight management programme devised in Germany fifteen years ago, which assesses your dietary needs through rigorous blood analysis and any medical conditions you may have. An individual nutrition plan is then formulated, recommending the exact foods your body requires as well as the combinations in which to eat them. Ludwig explains the essential purpose of the diet, as the name suggests, is to bring the body back into metabolic balance by restoring hormone balance through reduced insulin levels and an increase in lean muscle. The plan really is a return to basics, advocating three square meals a day with no snacking in between, to allow the body to repair and burn fat. With meal plans consisting of natural, nutritious ingredients from all the essential food groups, the body is fuelled and nourished sufficiently so there is no need for any dietary transgressions or 'yo-yoing'. It seems like a logical and realistic formula for us all. Less of a diet and a more considered approach to the way we eat, perhaps healthy eating really is simpler than we realise.

www.metabolic-balance.co.uk
www.nutrition-works.eu

METABOLIC BALANCE'S 8 GOLDEN RULES.

1. Eat three meals a day. Follow your plan carefully: do not eat more, do not eat less, and do not eat anything other than what is included on your personal food list.

2. After each meal, take a break of at least five hours before starting your next meal.

3. Do not allow any single meal to last longer than 60 mins.

4. Always begin each meal with one or two bites of protein.

5. Choose one type of protein per meal. Select another protein item from another protein group, for the remaining meals of the day.

6. Finish your evening meal by 9 pm.

7. Over the course of the day, drink ensure that you drink the amount of water that has been calculated for your body. This is usually around 35ml per kg body weight.

8. Eat one apple a day with a meal.

Cider Goes Suave

Written by James Hood

A REPORTED ONE IN FOUR OF US WILL NOW CHOOSE FIZZY FRUIT BEVERAGE CIDER OVER A COLD BEER. SO WE SPOKE TO THE TEAM AT ONE OF LONDON'S TRENDIEST BARS AND AN INDEPENDENT PRODUCER FROM THE ENGLISH COUNTRYSIDE TO FIND OUT WHAT MAKES CIDER SO SPECIAL.

You know a drink is becoming a premium product when Stella Artois releases an ad campaign and coins the phrase 'not cider, cidre' (pronounced seedr).

The Belgian brand, known for an unwavering dedication to perfection, launched its own cider range in 2011, confirming what many of us had already come to believe; cider has arrived. Official reports claim the drink is steaming towards the billion-pound-industry milestone, with more and more of us choosing to replace our usual beverage with something a little more fruity. Market research company Mintel believes that sales will reach £3.7 billion per year by 2017, with both apple and pear varieties being the firm favourites.

What makes the rise of cider as a popular drink so surprising, is that it's been around for centuries. Across the globe, and especially in our beloved West Country, farmers and their ancestors have thought nothing of fermenting their apples to create a refreshing alcoholic drink. Perhaps that's why, until recently, it's had a reputation for being reserved for country bumpkins, nature lovers and hippies. So what changed, and why is this cider's time to shine?

The Zeller Townhouse

"APPLES HAVE BEEN GROWN IN ENGLAND SINCE LONG BEFORE THE ROMANS ARRIVED... IT IS ONLY RIGHT THAT IT IS FINALLY HAVING ITS MOMENT AND FINDING ITS WAY INTO ELEGANT DRINKING ESTABLISHMENTS."

Matteo Malisan, bar manager at London's stylish Zetter Townhouse, thinks it has a lot to do with negative health implications of some other alcoholic drinks. "People have started drinking cider in higher volumes in recent years due to the fact that it is considered more healthy than beer, as well as having a lower glycaemic index than other forms of popular alcohol," Matteo told Food Stories Magazine.

The cynics among you are probably thinking there is something else at play here. After all, how many twenty or thirty-somethings are concerned about their waistlines on a Saturday night out? And they are part of the demographic, by all accounts, ordering cider by the gallon. Could it have anything to do with the brands convincing us it's the must-have drink? Looking at the shelves in the cider section of the off license, or even at some of the labels on more authentic, natural brands like Green and Pleasant (more on them later), the packaging has modernised - from stuffy to smart. As Matteo comments: "More than the health reasons, cider is currently enjoying a revival quite simply due to relentless marketing and PR campaigns on behalf of brands and their larger umbrella corporations."

As well as the consumers putting a 12-case of cider in their trolley, the success of the drink has also been fuelled by people like Matteo. Accomplished and talented bar men or cocktail masters have begun incorporating cider into their creations, which only adds to its kudos. Matteo told us: "We have chosen to serve certain ciders, due to their versatility and flavour profiles. Here at Zetter Townhouse we use Breton for its fruitiness, full flavour and dry finish. This is the cider that we use in a cocktail called Somerset Sour. It was chosen for the flavour profile it provides as well as the fact that it fits seamlessly into the liquid, allowing for a cocktail that contains multiple layers of apple flavour, acting as a crown for a most regal drink indeed."

Despite its new status on the cocktail menus of London's elite bars and being enjoyed by the Made in Chelsea set, cider retains a humble sense of heritage here in England. The tradition of making it is being kept alive respectfully by small, independent businesses like Green and Pleasant.

The company's founder, Andy Murray, told Food Stories Magazine: "The rise in interest in cider and artisanal products has given us a wonderful platform to showcase our small batch producers who previously might never have been discovered by cider lovers. Consumers are now incredibly savvy in what they're looking for and they have more choice than ever. The one thing they tend to agree on is that they are searching for the purest and most delicious product possible with ingredients that are locally sourced to where the drinks are produced. Our cider is simply made from apples alone and the

fruit travels just four miles from the tree to the press. It is then washed, mashed, pressed and left alone."

The skill is in the blending and this is all done by taste, by master cider maker, Brian Wilce. "We've been making cider on the farm for decades, with six generations of cider makers. We use 34 varieties of apples – all genuine Herefordshire cider apples. Our cider is a pure juice product, there's no need to add anything but time: seven months fermentation followed by carbonation." Founder of Green and Pleasant, Andy Murray continued "We're a fairly young business and so far, we don't export Green & Pleasant. But in the last month alone, we've had enquiries from Germany, France, Italy and the USA so we're confident that English cider is going cosmopolitan."

If all this cider talk has you gasping for a glass, Matteo has some advice on how it should be served. "In our opinion, cider should be consumed without ice. We believe in treating cider more like a white wine. We would never advise it be consumed at room temperature as this could make it appear musty on the palate. For us the optimal service temperature for a cider should be around 10 to 11 degrees centigrade so that it doesn't lose its crisp character and to close off a little of the sweetness."

1st page: Barmen at the Zetter Townhouse.
2nd page: The Zetter Townhouse front door.
Previous page: Green and Pleasant graphics.
This page: Andy Murray, co founder,
of Green and Pleasant.

www.thezettertownhouse.com
www.green-and-pleasant.com

Get Children to the Table Hungrier

Written by Susannah Prain

THE ONGOING DEBATE OF HOW AND WHAT TO FEED CHILDREN RAGES ON, CAN WE ADJUST THE HABITS AND LIFESTYLES OF MODERN FAMILIES WITH SOME SIMPLE AND REALISTIC CHANGES TO EVERYDAY LIFE?

The cautionary adage "don't spoil your appetite" was one uttered by scores of parents through the generations but what about the current generation? Are parents still concerned about ensuring children come to the table hungry or are they more nonchalant about mealtimes? It is clear eating habits have changed in recent years. Partly due to cheaper and more convenient food but lifestyle also plays a part. People are leading busier lives, with less emphasis on routine and a more informal attitude to meals. Nutritional adviser, Alice Fotheringham of the UK charity, the Food Education Foundation, says today parents regularly struggle with meal times. So the charity works in partnership with the National Childbirth Trust

and delivers practical advice to parents through food education workshops. Evidence suggests many children aren not getting the diet they require, missing out on essential food groups that would usually be served at meal times.

Snacking unhealthily between meals has reached epidemic proportions in the West due to the accessibility of 'junk' and fast foods, contributing to a rise in obesity, diabetes and tooth decay. It is not just older children having the means to procure these foods but also parents providing them for their children. Many modern parents are guilty of falling into a 'snack or snap' trap. A whinging child, setting a parent's nerves on edge, can be easily pacified with an oral distraction in the form of a snack. Fotheringham suggests "If children are hungry between meals, there are plenty of healthy foods to give them in modest sizes, as a boost, raw vegetables being a favourite of mine. Adding foods that are high in protein such as nut and seed butters, natural yoghurt and houmous will also keep blood sugars balanced and children sated for longer without filling them up." Fotheringham advocates involving children in meal preparation from a young age. "Even if it's just stirring or counting and weighing, children are learning about food, textures and flavours and even improving vital skills such as problem solving and coordination. Then they will be happy to sit down and eat what they helped to create." Taking that one stage further, to the source of healthy food, getting children involved in growing plants is a fun way of connecting them with the food on their plate. An easy example of this would be a mushroom kit from The Espresso Mushroom Company which can be grown indoors. Fotheringham believes that we have lost touch with 'mindful eating', the ability to focus on and appreciate the food in front of us without being distracted by extraneous stimuli such as screens. The message from previous generations still rings true, three square meals a day and sending children out to play, however parents today need support in choosing the right foods for their families and avoiding the negative influences that modern day life can present.

www.foodeducationfoundation.org.uk

1st page: Lorenza, Estelle and Greta getting involved with the food they eat. This page: The Breakfast Express from Such & Such www.suchandsuch.co

TOP TEN HEALTHY SNACKS

1. Frozen watermelon.
2. Corn thins.
3. Organic low sugar yoghurt.
4. Nuts, with caution to allergies.
5. Rye cracker thins.
6. Sugar free oat cakes.
7. Popcorn.
8. Vegetable crisps.
9. Houmous and vegetable sticks.
10. Fresh fruit.

TOP 10 INVOLVING TECHNIQUES

1. Involvement is everything, let children help and cook in the kitchen.
2. Give them the shopping list when food shopping, let them get the ingredients.
3. Sit down together at mealtimes.
4. At restaurants, pick from the starter menu for children instead of the kids menu.
5. Grow your own, giving children the responsibility of looking after their own plants.
6. Visit a 'pick your own' fruit and veg farm.
7. Make a mess, let children put their own meals together, likes tortilla wraps, rolls, salad etc.
8. Colour charts, let children choose a colour for every day of the week and then incorporate their chosen vegetables and fruit to match.
9. Go Global, pick a country and find a recipe to match.
10. Take children to Farmers Markets where they can get involved in trying and tasting.

fruit
+
veg
=
health

The Rise of British Charcuterie

Written by Susannah Prain

NO LONGER DO WE HAVE TO TURN TO EUROPE FOR OUR CHARCUTERIE, WE SPEAK TO THOSE LEADING THE CHARGE IN HOME GROWN CURING AND THE IMPORTANCE OF KEEPING IT BRITISH.

Alan Bartlett, is a third generation butcher from the New Forest. Twelve years ago there was a meeting of minds when he and James Golding, chef director at The Pig had the idea of curing local meat. "James was opening a packet of imported charcuterie and he turned to me and said, 'we have such great local meat, why aren't we curing it?' So, it was decided, James would come up with the recipes, I would do the rest." After frequent trips to Italy and plenty of trial and error, the pair gradually perfected the recipes and A Pinch of Salt Curing was born.

The process of dry curing meat involves minimal ingredients: salt; sugar; seasoning; air and time. "We use the whole carcass, loin for the lomo, shoulder for the coppa, belly for the pancetta, legs for the 'karma' ham and the trimmings for chorizo and salami," explains Bartlett. He typically favours Middle Whites for his pork as they lend themselves well to the curing process, being the ideal size and characteristically sweeter in flavour. Several branches of The Pig are now rearing Tamworths, Gloucester Old Spots and Saddlebacks which also provide Bartlett with meat to create the Italian style 'salami'. "Then we heard of a lad breeding wild boar down the road in the Forest," says Bartlett excitedly. "Wild boar disappeared from the New Forest nearly three centuries ago and James Burgess is the first farmer to reinstate them." The ancient and once prevalent practice of pannage

"WE WANT TO PRESERVE AS MUCH OF THE NATURAL FLAVOUR OF THE VENISON AS POSSIBLE"

allow farmers like Burgess to release their pigs and boar during the autumn to feed on fallen acorns and nuts in the forest. The effects are two-fold; an essential part of forest management, it reduces the risk of cattle and wild ponies ingesting the abundant acorns and nuts that may be harmful to them, and it also results in imparting a delicious nutty sweetness to the flavour of the boar.

Another curing company to use wild meat for their products are Great Glen Charcuterie. Based in the Scottish highlands Jan, a former Estate Manager, and his wife Anja source venison from local estates to make air-dried products such as bresaola, chorizo, green pepper salami, mustard seed salami and pepperoni. "We want to preserve as much of the natural flavour of the venison as possible," explains Anja. The deer roam the hillsides, grazing on heather, shrubs and grass, living as wild and naturally as nature intended. As a result, the venison is very tasty as well as healthy for the consumer, being lean and rich in iron, B vitamins and protein.

Since 2015 Cannon & Cannon, a leading UK distributor of British Cured Meat, have been running Meat School. Here you can learn during hands-on classes how to carry out the forgotten art of curing and preparing meats, classes which include 'classic curing' and 'make your own bacon.' Included within the course is study of the background of the product along with knife, curing and knotting skills. Talks and tasting sessions are also available.

With the growth in appreciation of quality and taste, an awareness of the provenance of our food and a greater sense of responsibility to the environment, we should all be looking to more sustainable and balanced meat rearing methods.

The message is keep it local and go wild.

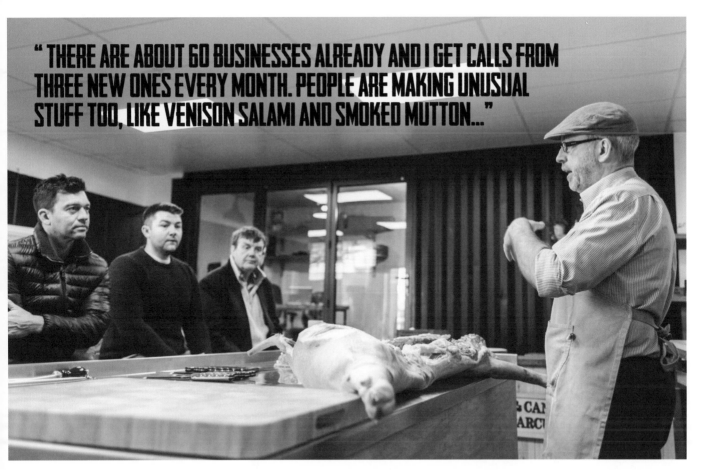

"THERE ARE ABOUT 60 BUSINESSES ALREADY AND I GET CALLS FROM THREE NEW ONES EVERY MONTH. PEOPLE ARE MAKING UNUSUAL STUFF TOO, LIKE VENISON SALAMI AND SMOKED MUTTON..."

Food Stories chatted to the Meat School founders and they promised us that after attending the meat school classes you would never look at super market salami or a pack of air dried ham in the same way again.

www.apinchofsaltcuring.co.uk
www.greatglencharcuterie.com
www.cannonandcannon.com

MEAT SCHOOL by CANNON & CANNON

Food Provenance

Written by James Hood

INCREASINGLY THE HISTORY AND AUTHENTICITY OF A PRODUCT IS AS IMPORTANT AS THE TASTE, FOOD STORIES INVESTIGATES TWO COMPANIES FOR WHOM ANONYMITY IS NOT AN OPTION.

On the supermarket shelf, the packages for Taylors of Harrogate coffee are boldly stamped with three options; Brazil, Guatemala or Columbia. Customers browsing are in no doubt where each of the tea and coffee company's products originated, but why does this matter to us? It seems it gives us more certainty as consumers of the quality and authenticity of goods - and it's something we're demanding more of from brands.

Over the last couple of years, understanding the provenance of food, a word derived from the French 'provenir', which means 'to come forth' or 'originate', has become vital for many shoppers before they buy. 2013's horse meat scandal highlighted how important it is to be able to trust the manufacturers that make the produce we consume. And in turn we've seen a plethora of marketing campaigns designed to reassure us of the credibility of the brands we love, or might spend our money on.

It doesn't have to be solely about our health, however. Increasingly as consumers we are bombarded with options, whether it's at the farmer's market or Marks and Spencer. So finding out more about the things we buy can simply make eating or drinking them more enjoyable. There are 10 different mustards, a dozen options for granola and countless kale soups. So is it any wonder we crave an affinity with a brand, a little history or background story to help us choose?

For Ole Hansen, owner of Hansen & Lydersen, it was a lack of quality that inspired him to bring exceptional smoked salmon from the Nordic seas to the UK. The Norwegian had grown up witnessing his parents and grandparents catching, smoking and preparing salmon - he tells the story beautifully on the company website. The taste was exceptional and undeniably better than much of the salmon available in our stores. So after spending time living in London, Ole decided to bring his great grandfather's methods of sourcing and preparing salmon to the city.

Today, the company operates from Stoke Newington in North London, where Ole and his team imports the salmon before it is hand-filleted and hand-salted using a family recipe devised by his great grandfather, fishmonger Lyder-Nilsen Lydersen, in 1923. After that the fish are hung and slowly cold-smoked in a brick kiln, where it moves in the wind for 12 hours.

"If you think about it, the health of a salmon when it's alive; the way it lives, and what it feeds on, is going to affect the taste," says Hansen. "So you want it to come from the best possible environment. Our salmon is caught from a sustainable farm in the extreme wilderness, between the Norwegian Sea and the North Atlantic Ocean. And we know that the salmon is fed on only the highest quality fish food from local fish stores. There's nothing artificial added. We also make a promise to ensure we prepare it within 48 hours of being fished."

Delivering food from its source to the plate in as short a time as possible is not a new craze. Ensuring food like meat, and other perishables such as fruit, are fresh and still edible by the time consumers get them home has been important to suppliers for decades. But now brands that truly care about food provenance are taking

"IF YOU THINK ABOUT IT, THE HEALTH OF A SALMON WHEN IT'S ALIVE; THE WAY IT LIVES, AND WHAT IT FEEDS ON, IS GOING TO AFFECT THE TASTE."

things a step further, preparing foods in a way that ensures the best possible taste for the end customer. Ole added: "Our work isn't over when the fish arrives here in London. It would be easy for us to box it immediately and not prepare it in the way I was shown as a young boy. Instead it's important to me that everything is done properly. We only wrap the salmon in grease-proof paper, to retain the quality. There's no plastic-covered or vacuum-packed salmon, which would taint the flavour."

Taking 'traceable' food quite literally is Primal Meats, a business that supplies meat solely from farms that rear animals to high standards directly to consumers, online. The company doesn't just focus on where its produce has come from. It makes it simple for customers to find out, too. By scanning a bar code on the packaging, customers are directed to a web page that shows them where the meat was sourced and gives details including age and sex of the animal it came from.

The demand for more information about the food we consume is driving producers and suppliers to not only find sustainable, responsible sources but to also tell us about them. In order to build a following - a customer base that continues to come back time after time, we're hearing more about the lengths producers go to for quality. And we're only too happy to listen.

What might seem like a more costly way to do business is actually building brand loyalty among customers. Hansen has the final word. "We could definitely cut costs way down. There are businesses out there that will find ways of saving money, or squeezing more profit from what they do. We refuse to compromise in that way, simply because it is not what's best for the product or our customer."

www.hansen-lydersen.com
www.primalmeats.co.uk

Food Stories Recipes...

IN THIS SECTION YOU WILL FIND FIFTY RECIPES EACH CELEBRATING A RARE FOOD BRAND. ALL OF THE RARE FOOD BRANDS ARE GREAT TASTE WINNERS FROM 2015. USE THE MEAL PLANNER AT THE BEGINING TO PLAN QUICK DISHES, IDEAL FOR ENTERTAINING.

Mackerel

ILLUSTRATIONS SUPPLIED BY WWW.SIVELLINK.DK

FOOD STORIES

Powered by

great taste ®

Canapés and Small Plates

TEMPURA OYSTERS AND CHILLI JAM

PREP: 15 MINS
COOK: 5 MINS

RED CABBAGE AND FETA SWEET SALAD

PREP: UNDER 30 MINS

PROPER MACKEREL PATE

PREP: UNDER 30 MINS

AVOCADO CHEESE SABLE CANAPÉS

PREP: UNDER 15 MINS

AMALFI BEER AND LEMON SORBET

PREP: UNDER 30 MINS

TRADITIONAL TURKISH FLATBREADS

PREP: 30 MINS
COOK: UNDER 30 MINS

LARGE AND HAPPY RICOTTA CROSTINIS

PREP: UNDER 15 MINS

WHITE BEAN DIP WITH BLACK GARLIC GARNISH

PREP: UNDER 30 MINS

FRESH FISH TACOS

PREP: 30 MINS
COOK: UNDER 30 MINS

SUMMERY GIN LOLLIPOPS

PREP: UNDER 30 MINS

FOOD STORIES

Powered by

Lunches

VEGETARIAN FRITTATA

PREP: 5 MINS
COOK: 25 MINS

BLACKENED PORK TACOS

PREP: 30 MINS
COOK: UNDER 1 HR

TIPSY TROUT FILLETS

PREP: UNDER 30 MINS
COOK: OVERNIGHT

GARDEN TART

PREP: 30 MINS
COOK: 1 HR

WILD AND CREAMY PORCINI PIE

PREP: 1 HR
COOK: 1 HR

NORTH AFRICAN SALAD

PREP: UNDER 30 MINS
COOK: 30 MINS

MIDDLE EASTERN STEAMED FISH

PREP: UNDER 30 MINS
COOK: 15 MINS

SALMON AND SEAWEED RAMEN

PREP: UNDER 15 MINS
COOK: UNDER 15 MINS

SALAMI STRUDEL

PREP: UNDER 30 MINS
COOK: UNDER 1 HR

CAMPS BAY BILTONG CITRUS SALAD

PREP: UNDER 15 MINS

FOOD STORIES

Powered by

great taste®

Suppers

HEARTY SPRING LAMB WITH FARRO

PREP: 30 MINS
COOK: 2 HRS

PORK BELLY WITH SWEET & SOUR SLAW

PREP: UNDER 30 MINS
COOK: 2 HRS

WILD VENISON

PREP: UNDER 15 MINS
COOK: UNDER 15 MINS

CIDER BRAISED CHICKEN

PREP: UNDER 30 MINS
COOK: UNDER 45 MINS

INDIAN STREET STYLE CHAPATI

PREP: UNDER 30 MINS
COOK: UNDER 15 MINS

ESPRESSO RUBBED MAN STEAK

PREP: 30 MINS
COOK: 1.5 HRS

OIL INFUSED SALMON

PREP: UNDER 15 MINS
COOK: UNDER 30 MINS

HONEY GLAZED PORK FILLET & RHUBARB

PREP: UNDER 15 MINS
COOK: UNDER 1 HR

SPRING POACHED LAMB

PREP: UNDER 30 MINS
COOK: OVER 1 HOUR

COD, HAM AND CAPERS

PREP: UNDER 15 MINS
COOK: UNDER 15 MINS

FOOD STORIES

Desserts

CRUNCHY NAUGHTY RHUBARB TRIFLE

PREP: UNDER 30 MINS
COOK: UNDER 30 MINS

MARRAKESH MERINGUES

PREP: UNDER 30 MINS
COOK: 1.5 HRS

NO-BAKE YOGURT CHEESECAKE

PREP: UNDER 1HR
COOK: CHILL OVERNIGHT

MADAGASCAR MILK CHOCCIE POTS

PREP: UNDER 15 MINS
COOK: UNDER 30 MINS

M'HENCHA WITH CARDAMOM CREME

PREP: UNDER 15 MINS

POSH PADDINGTON TART

PREP: 1 HR
COOK: UNDER 30 MINS

CITRUS AND THYME POSSET

PREP: UNDER 30 MINS
COOK: UNDER 1 HR

ORANGE & NOUGAT GELATI

PREP: UNDER 30 MINS

CHOCOLATE FILLED RASPBERRIES

PREP: UNDER 15 MINS
COOK: UNDER 15 MINS

SMOKED LAYER CAKE

PREP: UNDER 1 HR
COOK: 2 HRS

FOOD STORIES

Powered by

great taste®

Pocket Feasts and Cake

NUTTY BREAKFAST BARS

PREP: **UNDER 15 MINS**
COOK: **UNDER 30 MINS**

LUCUMA LAMINGTONS

PREP: **UNDER 30 MINS**
COOK: **UNDER 1 HR**

POCKET PASTIES

PREP: **UNDER 15 MINS**
COOK: **UNDER 30 MINS**

CLASSIC BRITISH CIDER APPLE JELLY

PREP: **UNDER 30 MINS**
COOK: **15 MINS**

SUNDRIED FIGGY PIZZA

PREP: **UNDER 15 MINS**
COOK: **UNDER 30 MINS**

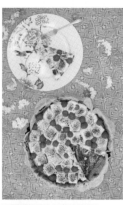

TORCHED MALLOW CAKE

PREP: **UNDER 30 MINS**
COOK: **UNDER 45 MINS**

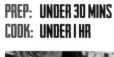

JASMINE LOAF CAKE

PREP: **UNDER 1 HOUR**
COOK: **UNDER 1 HOUR**

ZESTY MEAD BUNDT CAKE

PREP: **UNDER 1 HOUR**
COOK: **UNDER 1 ½ HOURS**

MASCARPONE AND COCOA COOKIES

PREP: **35 MINS**
COOK: **20 MINS**

SOY DOUGHNUTS

PREP: **1 HR**
COOK: **1 HR**

Canapés and Small Plates...

HERE ARE TEN RECIPES THAT ARE WONDERFULLY THEMED FOR SPRING AND SUMMER - SMALL IS BEAUTIFUL!

Peas

ILLUSTRATIONS SUPPLIED BY WWW.SIVELLINK.DK

RED CHILLI KITCHEN LTD

The story begins in Vietnam, Thao Nguyen was born in Phuoc Long, South Vietnam. Although her family was living through the Vietnam War, life was good until the mid seventies, when the North Vietnamese took their revenge on those who had shown any allegiance towards the South Vietnamese government and the Americans. Thao's father, a translator for America's Special Forces, was sent to a "re-education" camp and life for her family became unbearable. In 1984, at the age of 12, Thao escaped on a small fishing boat. She spent 10 days drifting at sea until she was rescued and taken to Indonesia. After seven months in a refugee camp, Thao was resettled in Denmark. Today Thao lives in Suffolk with her family, where she runs Red Chilli Kitchen so that others can taste the delicious recipes her mother cooked in her Vietnamese kitchen.

Vietnamese cuisine is light, fresh, fragrant and full of colour and natural flavours and all this is in Red Chilli Kitchen's award winning tomato chilli jam blended with lemongrass and ginger. So as they say in Vietnam "An Ngon" - eat well!

www.therarebrandmarket.co.uk/ redchillikitchen

RED CHILLI KITCHEN

Oysters supplied by www.keenanseafood.com

RED CHILLI KITCHEN
VIETNAMESE TOMATO CHILLI JAM

PREP: 15 MINS   **SERVES:** 2

COOK: 5 MINS

INGREDIENTS

4 oysters, shucked
and cleaned
flour, for dusting
oil, for deep-frying
Red Chilli Kitchen
Tomato Chilli Jam

Tempura batter:
50g plain flour
50g cornflour
1 tsp baking powder
200ml ice-cold
sparkling water
salt and freshly
ground black pepper

METHOD

To make tempura batter, mix all the dry ingredients
in a large bowl. Slowly add in the ice cold sparkling
water a little at a time, until you have a smooth batter,
about single cream consistancy. Transfer the batter to a
container and keep it chilled.

Rinse the oysters under running cold water and dry.
Use shucking knife to open carefully. Roll the oysters
in the dusting flour.

Heat the oil in a small, high sided pan. To check if the
oil is hot enough use a cube of bread: it should turn
golden brown in 30 seconds. When ready, dip two of
the oysters in the batter and carefully place in the oil.
After 20–30 seconds, the oysters should be crisp and
brown. Remove and repeat. Place the battered oysters
back in the shells and serve with the tomato chilli jam
for dipping.

FRED AND BEX

Fred and Bex make traditional handmade fruit vinegars in the tranquil Lincolnshire countryside, using a family recipe which had been passed down from generation to generation. For over seven years, using a secret blend of whole fruit, white wine vinegars and sugar they have been crafting their products.

They are passionate about what they do and recommend their vinegars to anyone wanting to give an edge to anything from salad dressings, syrups and cake icing to adding great swigs to casseroles and tagines - giving favourite dishes an old fashioned kick with a natural, rich taste. You can find lots of great recipe ideas on their website. The Fred and Bex Raspberry and Blackberry Fruit Vinegars won a total of three gold stars at the Great Taste awards in 2015.

www.therarebrandmarket.co.uk/fredandbex

FRED AND BEX SWEET RASPBERRY VINEGAR

PREP: UNDER 30 MINS   **SERVES:** 4 MAIN 6 SIDE DISH

INGREDIENTS

2 -3 tablespoons sweet Fred and Bex raspberry vinegar
3 tablespoons argan oil
1 small red onion, peeled, thinly sliced
salt and pepper
6-8 pitted dates

1/2 red cabbage, cut into thin ribbons
large handful of chopped parsley
4oz. feta cheese
1-2 tablespoons of toasted sesame/ pumpkin seeds

METHOD

Place the chopped cabbage and sliced onion in a large bowl and pour over the oil and vinegar.

Mix together well and then season with salt and pepper. Leave to sit whilst you prepare the other ingredients.

Gently mix in the dates, feta and parsley and finally sprinkle the toasted seeds on top.

This salad is a great on its own or with other ingredients as part of a summer lunch. But note that the oil and vinegar will gently soften the salad over time so if you like that extra crunch prepare at the last minute.

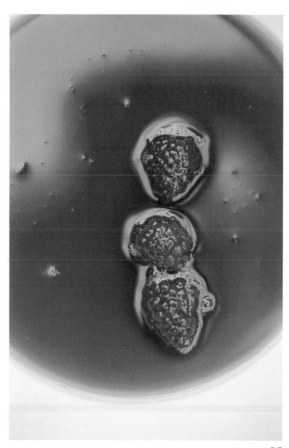

PETER'S YARD

Peter's Yard, want to bring the very best of Swedish baking to the rest of the world. The story began when founders, Ian and Wendy set out on a mission to discover the best Swedish bakeries and bring some of their favourite bread, cakes and biscuits back to the UK. On their journey they visited Peter Ljunquist's Swedish bakery, Peter's Yard. There they drank coffee, chatted to Peter and enjoyed "fika". They also discovered the most delicious crispbread (knäckebröd) they had ever eaten. It was simply too good to remain confined to one small bakery, so they decided to work with Peter, to make this authentically Swedish, delicious crispbread available across the UK.

The team used naturally fermenting sourdough, Shipton Mill organic flour and the very best, natural ingredients. Recommendations spread by word of mouth and soon, the little wavy, golden crispbreads started to be selected by chefs at Michelin starred restaurants and began to win plenty of awards. From a cautious start, making just 50kg of crispbread a week (that's not even enough to fill one small bakery van), they are now producing fifty times that much in order to keep up with the growing demand from food lovers who claim to be "addicted" to their crisp texture and subtle flavour.

www.therarebrandmarket.co.uk/petersyard

PETER'S YARD ARTISAN CRISPREAD

PREP: UNDER 30 MINS **SERVES:** 4 AS A STARTER

INGREDIENTS

250g hot-smoked mackerel fillet
25g unsalted butter
1/2 clove garlic, peeled and crushed
1 tea spoon of horseradish
pinch of cayenne pepper
2 tbsp crème fraîche
squeeze of lemon juice
freshly ground black pepper
1 packet Peter's Yard Artisan Crispbread

METHOD

Peel the skin of the fish and then flake the mackerel
into a large bowl, taking care to remove any bones.

Put the butter in a small pan with the garlic and
cayenne pepper. Heat until the butter is just
simmering, then pour over the fish and let it sink in.

Add the crème fraîche, a squeeze of lemon and a
teaspoon of horseradish (if you would like more of a
kick add more than a teaspoon), season generously
with black pepper. Give it a good mix, remembering
the more you stir and blend together the smoother the
texture will be.

Serve with Peter's Yard's wonderful Artisan
Crispbread.

THE PEA GREEN BOAT

The Pea Green Boat is a small artisan food company based just outside Edinburgh in Cockenzie, East Lothian and is run by Maddy Corbin. The company specialises in making unique and delicious cheese sablés. The original recipe for these delicious biscuits comes from Hugh Corbin (Maddy's dad). He undertook the challenge to make the best cheese biscuit in the world. On the panel of judges were Maddy, her mum Pam, sister Philippa, plus any passersby. There were many trials and tribulations, and a few dead ends. Finally he landed on the recipe - all were in agreement, these were truly the best cheese biscuits in the world. So when Maddy started her business in 2011, making goods in her home kitchen and selling them at markets, the cheese sablés were an obvious product for her to make and sell. The original award winning cheese variety is joined by cumin, and fennel and chilli sablés. Hugh Corbin regularly checks the quality!

www.therarebrandmarket.co.uk/thepeagreenboat

AVOCADO CHEESE SABLE CANAPÉS

CHEESE SABLES THE PEA GREEN BOAT

PREP: UNDER 15 MINS   **SERVES:** SEVERAL CANAPÉS

ASSEMBLY: UNDER 15 MINS

INGREDIENTS

2 packets The Pea Green Boat cheese sables
225g cream cheese, take out of the fridge to soften
15g dill, chopped finely, plus more to garnish
2 spring onion stalks, finely chopped
1 clove garlic, finely chopped
1 avocado, peeled and sliced
1 tsp lemon juice
Freshly ground black pepper

METHOD

After the cream cheese has been left to soften for a while mix it together with the garlic and pepper into a bowl, make sure the garlic is well blended and not in any clumps.

Lightly spread the sables with the seasoned cream cheese and top with the avocado. Squeeze a few drops of lemon to stop the avocado from browning. Garnish with spring onion and dill for a beautifully tasty and delicate canapé. Experiment with different herb toppings, such as mint and basil for a wonderfully aromatic selection.

SAVOUR BRITISH FARMHOUSE BEER

Farmhouse beers were traditionally brewed by farmers in winter time to be served as a light refreshing drink to the workers, during the long days of the summer harvest. Savour British Farmhouse Beer, was founded in 2013 by Sandy Kirkpatrick, a farmer's son from Scotland. Kirkpatrick has two passions in his life: farming and beer. Launching Savour is a satisfying culmination of the two, and the result is an outstanding range of award winning beers created for those longing an escape to the British countryside.

Kirkpatrick worked with a leading English sparkling wine producer to create their Sparkling Beer Brut. The beer is matured in the bottle before being riddled and disgorged using the traditional method to remove the yeast sediment. An elegant floral and spicy aroma gives way to a luxurious, rich body and effervescent finish. A beer of truly exceptional character and one of only six beers in the world to be made using this traditional method. This lively tipple is a great example of how Savour British Beer is revitalising a traditional product to suit a modern marketplace.

www.therarebrandmarket.co.uk/savourbeer

SAVOUR

SPECIALIST BRITISH BEER

SAVOUR SPARKLING BRUT

PREP: UNDER 30 MINS   **SERVES:** 4-6

INGREDIENTS

500g caster sugar
500ml water
1 lemon, juice and
zest

1 lemon, sliced
350ml sparkling
Savour Sparkling Beer
Brut

METHOD

Firstly, if you are making this sorbet in a metal bowl, place it empty in the freezer to chill, at least the night before, as it helps to quicken the freezing process.

To make the syrup, put the sugar, water and lemon juice in a saucepan and bring to a simmer leaving it to reduce by a quarter.

When it has reached a slightly syrupy consistency, stir in the beer and lemon zest. Leave it to cool in the fridge. Transfer the liquid to a strong plastic or metal tub and put it in the freezer. After about an hour it will have frozen around the edges so beat vigorously to make a slush. Try to repeat maybe twice more and then leave the sorbet to freeze.

Move to the fridge about 20 minutes before serving so it has time to soften.

Serve with a slice or two of lemon.

FELIN TALGARTH MILL

Set in the Brecon Beacons National Park, the derelict Talgarth watermill's restoration story began in 2011, as part of the BBC's Village SOS programme. Five years on, and it is a thriving community enterprise milling stoneground flour, and run by a group of dedicated and passionate volunteers. This ancient flour mill has established a strong and award-winning brand, catching the eye of retailers and consumers alike.

Expectations and targets have been exceeded and the quality of the flour - and the baked goods made in the Mill's cafe - has resulted in a number of awards for the enterprise. 'Blawd o safon, o rym yr afon' - 'Quality flour from the power of the river' - it certainly is.
www.therarebrandmarket.co.uk/talgarthmill

TALGARTH MILL SEVEN SEEDS STRONG WHOLEMEAL FLOUR

PREP: 30 MINS   **SERVES:** 4

COOK: UNDER 30 MINS

INGREDIENTS

1 x 7g sachet instant dried yeast
300ml warm water
pinch of salt
1 tsp caster sugar
360g Talgarth Mill Seven Seeds Strong Wholemeal Flour

2 tbsp argan oil
75g baby spinach
75g baby kale
200g feta cheese, crumbled
lemon wedges, to serve
oil for brushing

METHOD

Combine water, yeast, salt and sugar in a bowl. Stir and let stand in a warm place for 5 minutes or until bubbles form on the surface.

Meanwhile place the flour into a separate bowl. Add yeast mixture and argan oil. Mix to form a soft dough, then turn out onto a lightly floured surface and knead until elastic (usually about 5 minutes).

Cut the dough into 4 and place on a greased baking tray. Cover with a clean tea towel. Stand in a warm place for 20 minutes or until dough roughly doubles in size

Roll each piece into a rectangle approx 30x45 cm. Place one quarter of the spinach and the baby kale over half of each rectangle. Top with feta and season with salt and pepper. Fold dough over to enclose filling. Press edges together to seal, creating the flatbread.

Preheat a heavy saucepan/griddle. Brush each flatbread with oil and cook for 2 to 3 minutes until it browns. Turn over and repeat. Remove and cut into quarters and serve with lemon wedges.

WHITE COTTAGE BAKERY

Helen Underwood, Head Baker at White Cottage Bakery, runs a microbakery and bread-making school from her farmhouse kitchen in Kingston, Cambridge. "With something as simple as bread, ingredients are key," she says. "We source the finest ingredients we can - locally, where possible, and 100% additive-free. The local miller provides our wonderful stoneground flour from grain grown on the Wimpole Estate, neighbouring the bakery. It's all about getting people back in touch with simple pleasures and forgotten tastes. I'm a great believer in Eat Less Bread! Better to buy one really great loaf and savour every last crust and crumb, than contribute to the vast quantity of sliced bread that is thrown into our bins each week."

www.therarebrandmarket.co.uk/ whitecottagebakery

5 SEED SOUR DOUGH LONQUE WHITE COTTAGE BAKERY

PREP: UNDER 15 MINS   **SERVES:** SEVERAL CROSTINIS

ASSEMBLY: UNDER 15 MINS

INGREDIENTS

1loaf sour dough bread
1 tbsp argan oil
250g ricotta
180g cream cheese
cracked pepper
lemon, juiced
Toppings of choice:
half avocado, sliced
6 strawberries, sliced

handful of blueberries
2 slices smoked salmon
cucumber, sliced
2 hard boiled eggs
handful of radishes, sliced
handful of cherry tomatoes, sliced

METHOD

These are quick, decorative and simply delicious.

Put the mixture of cream cheese and ricotta into a bowl and combine well. Season with the pepper and some lemon juice.

Slice the bread, finely, brush with oil and then toast until it is golden brown.

Spread toast with the ricotta mix and toppings of your choice. We used avocado, strawberries and blueberries, smoked salmon, egg, radish, tomato and finally sliced cucumber, a lovely mixture of sweet and savoury. Any wonderful salad vegetables and fruits would work well.

SOUTH WEST GARLIC FARM

It was 18 years ago that Mark Botwright, who owns the South West Garlic Farm in Dorset, switched from sheep farming to garlic growing. He had received some bulbs from his wife, Wendy, to grow in their vegetable garden and he was hooked. His idea for producing British Black Garlic came about to fill a gap in production over winter.

When Mark was looking for ways to make garlic products that were beyond the normal chutneys and pickles he came across a 4,000-year-old Korean recipe on the internet. It took him 14 months to perfect the garlic recipe which has been awarded two stars in The Great Taste awards. Following on that success he has launched Black Garlic Sea Salt and received another Great Taste award. Further products are being developed using this unique ingredient - chefs who applaud his black garlic include Nigella Lawson, Mark Hix and Yotam Ottolenghi.

www.therarebrandmarket.co.uk/ southwestgarlicfarm

South West Garlic Farm

SOUTH WEST GARLIC FARM BLACK GARLIC

PREP: UNDER 30 MINS   **SERVES:** 6

INGREDIENTS

3 (400g) tins cannellini beans
1 whole head black garlic, peeled
4 white garlic cloves, peeled and crushed
1 tbsp rapeseed oil
1/2 tsp fresh thyme, chopped
250ml organic double cream, warmed
salt
freshly ground black pepper to taste

METHOD

Drain 2 of the tins of cannellini beans and rinse them thoroughly in cold water. After they have drained blitz them in a food processor until they are smooth and pour the mixture into a serving bowl.

Add the crushed white garlic, chopped thyme and cream. Then place in the fridge to chill.

Drain and rinse the third tin of cannellini beans. Gently add to the mixture of white beans stirring carefully so they do not break up. Add seasoning to taste.

Finely chop the whole black garlic and sprinkle over the bean dip with a drizzle of oil - it will infuse and mix into the dip creating a deep soft garlicky flavour.

COOL CHILE CO.

After travelling around Mexico tasting and testing different foods, Dodie Miller started Cool Chile Co in 1993. The idea was simple: import the best dried chillies direct from Mexico.

Cool Chile Co wanted to provide the UK with the warm, earthy flavours and smells that instantly transport you to Mexico: salsas and sauces made with toasted dried chillies; tortillas fresh from the Comal. Mexican chocolate whipped into hot frothy drinks; Mexican oregano rubbed over pozole or black beans bubbling in a pot with epazote and fresh corn tortillas. These were the tastes and spiced sensations of Mexico.

The chillies come in three different forms: whole, diced or powdered. The corn tortillas are freshly made to order and are preservative and gluten free. All the sauces, from achiote to mole, are all made without preservatives, and the cocoa nibs are ground to make delicately spiced Mexican and Maya drinking chocolate.

www.therarebrandmarket.co.uk/coolchile

Hake supplied by www.keenanseafood.com

COOL CHILE COMPANY TORTILLA

PREP: 30 MINS   **SERVES: 4**

COOK: UNDER 30 MINS

INGREDIENTS

400g hake
1 tsp of cumin
1 tsp of paprika
1/2 tsp sea salt
1/4 tsp pepper
pinch of cayenne pepper
- if you like a little kick
8 Cool Chile Company
tortillas
Coleslaw:
3 large handfuls spring
cabbage, shredded

2 carrots, grated
2 spring onions, sliced
2 tbsp rapeseed oil
1 tbsp apple cider vinegar
1 tsp Dijon mustard
Salsa:
4 small tomatoes
1/4 red onion
2 jalapeños
1/2 lime, juiced
salt and pepper

Guacamole:
2 ripe avocados,
mashed
1/4 red onion

2 jalapeños
1/2 lime, juiced
salt and pepper

METHOD

Put the prepared cabbage, carrots and spring onions into salad bowl. In a jug whisk together the oil, vinegar, mustard and salt. Pour over salad and toss.

Salsa: dice tomatoes, onion and jalapeños, draining the excess liquid. Add lime juice and season. Guacamole: peel the avocados, and mash with a fork. Add finely diced onion and jalapeños to the avocado along with the lime juice and season.

Fish: rinse the hake under cold water and pat dry. Combine the cumin, paprika, sea salt and cayenne pepper together in a bowl and rub it all over the fish. Preheat a griddle pan and cook the fish on a medium heat for 4-5 minutes per side or until cooked dependent on thickness of fish.

Slightly scorch and warm the tortilla shells on the hot griddle about 3 minutes before fish is done. Assemble tortilla tower by starting with a tortilla, then coleslaw, fish, guacamole and salsa. Repeat and enjoy.

SIBLING DISTILLERY

Sibling Distillery is a gin distillery, based in Cheltenham since 2014 - the distillers are four siblings, all aged under 23. They produce a contemporary, smooth gin in a state of the art distillery made from glass and stainless steel, known as a 'crystal still' - the first of its kind in Europe. With an aim of introducing new gin drinkers to the spirit, and offering seasoned gin drinkers something new - the spirit is distilled and filtered like a premium vodka until the last step, ensuring absolute clarity and purity - a completely blank slate on which to build their flavours. This means they can use delicate and subtle botanicals when vapour infusing them on their carterhead distillery, giving the gin its signature softness that has made it such a success. With botanicals including fresh oranges, blueberries and Madagascan vanilla it offers some smoother, fruitier notes to compliment the traditional gin botanicals and create an amazingly refreshing drink.

www.therarebrandmarket.co.uk/siblingdistillery

SUMMERY GIN LOLLIPOPS

SIBLING TRIPLE DISTILLED GIN

PREP: UNDER 30 MINS   **ASSEMBLY:** OVERNIGHT

INGREDIENTS

175g raspberries
175g pomegranate arils
200g caster sugar
1 lemon

1 cucumber, sliced
500ml water
240ml Sibling Triple Distilled Gin

METHOD

Firstly slice the cucumber, either into ribbons or rounds and place in the lollipop moulds in the freezer (having the cucumber already frozen will help to distribute the rest of the fruit).

Simmer half the water, pomegranate arils and sugar for 8-10 minutes.

Leave to cool and then add the juice of one lemon, gin, raspberries and the rest of the water, leave this mixture to cool right down.

Pour into the lolly moulds, as quickly as possible, trying not to let too much fruit clump together. Preferably put into the freezer for overnight.

Remember that due to the alcohol content they will melt quickly so only take them out of the freezer at the last minute before serving.

OVER 20 TYPES OF ORGANIC FAIRTRADE TEA TO CHOOSE FROM!

QI TEA (QI FROM THE ANCIENT CHINESE MEANING "NATURAL ENERGY OF LIFE") WE HAVE THE UK'S LARGEST COLLECTION OF ORGANIC FAIRTRADE TEA.

www.qi-teas.com

Lunches...

IN THIS SECTION YOU WILL FIND TEN LUNCHES, A MIXTURE OF HOT AND COLD, FORMAL AND CASUAL, THAT WILL SUIT INDOOR AND OUTDOOR EATING FOR SPRING AND SUMMER.

Langoustine and Samphire

LYBURN FARMHOUSE CHEESE

In 1952 the Smales family bought a farm in Hampshire, and three Gurnsey cows: Faith, Hope and Charity. From that day to this the family has been milking cows twice a day, every day. Since then the family has grown, and so has the farm and the herd: fourth generation; 450 acres and 170 cows respectively.

Every day starts at 7am when the herd of Holstein-Friesian cows are milked. The cows produce 2,200 litres of milk. This is pasturised and rennet is added to create the nursery rhyme 'curds and whey.' Enter the cheesemaker, who uses his years of experience to create the magic, and by lunchtime the basic cheese is made.

The following morning the perfectly formed, moulded cheeses are taken to the brine tank for about 24 hours and then to the drying room. From here the cheeses are taken to the ripening room for around seven months to join the 8000 circles of cheese maturing at any one time. The moment of truth is in the tasting - each cheese will taste and smell slightly different. All the detail of the make is recorded, and the cheese is graded. Lyburn have been getting it right for decades, most recently with Stoney Cross, a mould-ripened cheese, made in the style of a Tomme De Savoie. Creamy and buttery in texture with sweet flavours and a distinctly earthy finish, it was awarded 3 Gold Stars at the 2015 Great Taste awards.
www.therarebrandmarket.co.uk/lyburncheese

VEGETARIAN FRITTATA

STONEY CROSS CHEESE LYBURN CHEESE

PREP: 5 MINS **SERVES:** 6

COOK: 25 MINS **PRE HEAT OVEN:** 175C

INGREDIENTS

2 tbsp melted butter
1 large onion, diced
225g button
mushrooms, de-
stemmed and diced
2 cloves garlic, diced
2 large handfuls baby
leaf spinach

6 eggs
200g Stoney Cross
cheese, grated
3 sprigs fresh
rosemary
salt and pepper

METHOD

In a large, oven-proof frying pan, melt butter, add the onion and saute until soft. Add mushrooms and garlic, cook for 3 to 4 minutes.

Add spinach and cook until wilted. Remove pan from heat.

In a bowl, whisk eggs until slightly frothy and add the grated cheese, mix together.

Pour mixture into mushroom pan and lightly stir to mix. Lay rosemary sprigs on top and season. Transfer to the oven and bake until eggs are firm, about 10 to 15 minutes. Serve hot.

REDHILL FARM FREE RANGE PORK

Farmers, Jane and Terry Tomlinson, set out 18 years ago to provide the people in Lincolnshire with access to the best tasting, highest quality free range pork straight from the people who produce it. The key to what they do well is giving their herd of Duroc cross Landrace pigs everything they need but, just as importantly, nothing they don't. They commit the extra time, effort, skill and expense needed to produce something of quality.

The free-range pork at Redhill Farm Free Range Pork is of exceptional quality, producing everything from matured, cured and smoked bacon and hams, to traditional Lincolnshire Sausages and Haslets, hand-raised pork pies and black pudding as well as their free-range pork. Redhill Farm Free Range Pork has won an astounding number of national awards as well as many fans, becoming suppliers to Jamie Oliver and James Martin and, sending Pork Pies to Lords' Cricket Ground. For over 10 years running their products have consistently scooped countless 1, 2 and 3 Star Gold's at the Great Taste awards including winning the 'Fine Food Oscar' for the region in 2014.

www.therarebrandmarket.co.uk/redhillfarm

REDHILL FARM®

FREE RANGE PORK

119

BLACKENED PORK TACOS

RED HILL FARM FREE RANGE PORK LOIN

PREP: 30 MINS   **SERVES:** 2-4

COOK: UNDER 1 HR   **PRE HEAT OVEN:** 180C

INGREDIENTS

4 x 160g pork loin
1 tsp allspice
3 tsp Cajun spice
1 tbsp rapeseed oil, extra for brushing
2 corn on the cob
8 taco shells
500g grated chesse
pickled jalapenos finely chopped

Salsa: 1 avocado freshly scooped
1 lime juice
extra limes to serve
180g broad beans blanched, peeled and roughly chopped
1 large handful of coriander, roughly chopped
250ml crème fraiche

METHOD

Preheat over to 180c. Mix the allspice and half of the Cajun Spice, into a paste with the oil and season. Coat the pork and set aside.

Heat a griddle pan over a medium heat and cook corn for 20 mins turning regularly until charred. Remove from heat. Cool, cut the kernels from the cob. Add the pork to the griddle pan and seal both sides. Place on a baking tray and bake in the oven for 20 mins. While the pork is cooking for the salsa: combine avocado, lime juice, broad beans, remaining Cajun spice and coriander leaves in a bowl and season with salt and pepper. Take out pork and slice.

On a baking tray lay the taco shells in a row and sprinkle over half the cheese, top with pork slices, some corn and jalapenos. Add the remaining cheese, place in the oven to warm through as per instructions, melting the cheese.

Gently remove tacos from the oven. Place on a large plate and serve the salsa on top with a dollop of crème fraiche.

CONKER SPIRIT

Apart from anything else, there's the beauty of the bottle which is boldly free from the constraints of tradition. The graphics - inspired by the eponymous childhood game are clever and fresh. Conker Spirit is Dorset's first gin distillery. Nestled in the sandy backstreets of Bournemouth, Conker Spirit quietly distils their award winning Dorset Dry gin in deliciously small, 70cl sixty bottle batches.

Conker Spirit is a labour of love for founder Rupert Holloway. His plan was for his team to do everything themselves. They know their product inside and out: they are the distillers; the bottlers; the labellers and even the botanical foragers. Dorset is key to Conker. As well as the location for the distillery, the gin uses New Forest spring water and botanicals unique to the area such as handpicked gorse flowers, elderberries and marsh samphire.

The Dorset Dry is a classic gin that is true to juniper, with the subtle incorporation of those intoxicating Dorset notes bringing bright and refreshing lighter notes to Conker. Neat, on the rocks, or as the kicker in a G&T this delicious spirit is topped off cleverly by a copper lid, a nod to reflect the traditional copper pot distilling process.

www.therarebrandmarket.co.uk/conkerspirit

CONKER
— SPIRIT — ®

DORSET
DRY | GIN

Trout supplied by www.chalkstreamfoods.co.uk

CONKER SPIRIT DORSET DRY GIN

PREP: UNDER 30 MINS   **SERVES:** 4-6

COOK: OVERNIGHT

INGREDIENTS

500g large trout fillet	Pickling Liquor:
500g caster sugar	200g caster sugar
500g table salt	100ml Conker Sprit
zest of 1 lemon	Dorset Dry Gin
10g cracked black	5g fennel seeds
pepper	handful parsley
10g juniper berries,	stalks, chopped
crushed	50ml white wine
100ml Conker Spirit	vinegar
Dorset Dry Gin	100ml white wine
	1 cucumber

METHOD

Using a pestle and mortar, or a blender crush the pepper and juniper berries together and then combine with the sugar, salt, gin and lemon zest.

Place the fish fillet in a large flat-bottomed dish, coat with the cure mix, making sure to smooth it all over the fish. Cover with clingfilm and leave in the fridge overnight.

Peel the cucumber into ribbons. Mix all the pickling liquor ingredients in a bowl. Add the cucumber and chill in the fridge.

The next day wipe excess cure from the fish and cut in to thin slices, serve with the pickled cucumber.

QUICKE'S

Mary Quicke's family have been farming in Newton St Cyres, Devon for over 450 years. Her parents, Sir John and Lady Prue built the dairy 25 years ago and it is still the heart of Home Farm. Set in 1500 acres of stunning countryside, the 500 strong herd turns lush Devonshire grass into perfect, rich creamy milk to make Quicke's award winning cheeses.

Quicke's use time-honoured methods and recipes passed down through generations to create outstanding cheddar: handmade, cloth-bound and slow matured. Month after month the artisanal cheesemakers use all their senses to discern the subtle shifts that mark out a good cheese from an exceptional one. All the cheeses are graded meticulously, using a century old grading scheme. Mary Quicke attends each grading personally to make sure each batch is as superb as the last.

Welfare of the cows, a three way cross breed of New Zealand Friesian, Swedish Red and Montbeliard, and excellent countryside stewardship lie at the very heart of the Quicke's philosophy. So, in addition to winning awards for her cheeses, her team maintain and restore 170 acres of hedges, orchards, beetle banks, ponds, footpaths and provide educational access so people can enjoy the countryside.

No two days are the same at Home Farm. The shifting seasons are observed and noted in a monthly Dairy Diary by Mary - a friendly mix of farming journal and wildlife reportage, with enthusiastic updates on cheese making and recipes from the farm kitchen.

www.therarebrandmarket.co.uk/quickes

QUICKE'S

DEVON
ENGLAND

QUICKE'S CLOTH GOAT MILK CHEESE

PREP: 30 MINS   **SERVES:** 6-8

COOK: 1 HR   **PRE HEAT OVEN:** 190C

INGREDIENTS

3 slices thick cut smoked bacon, chopped and cooked

140g Quicke's goat milk cheese

3 large eggs

285g Greek yogurt

60ml double cream

25g minced chives

1 bunch of asparagus, woody bits removed

1 pack of puff pastry

METHOD

Divide the asparagus, one third cut into 30cm pieces, one third shaved into ribbons and the remainder left whole.

Roll out to the pastry to about the thickness of a £1 coin and lay over a 30cm tart tin pressing the pastry into the corners. Put in the freezer until needed.

Putting asparagus and one third of the chives aside combine all ingredients (except the bacon) into a large bowl and whisk until the eggs and cheese are well mixed. Add the cut aspargus to the mixture and pour into the prepared crust and then top with the whole asparagus spears.

Bake for about 45 minutes until the centre is set and the crust is golden brown.

While the tart is cooling, cook the bacon. When cooked set aside and using the same pan lightly fry the shaved asparagus for a minute or two. Season well.

Top the tart with the shaved asparagus, cooked bacon, remaining chives and some fresh grated goats cheese. Serve warm.

GET FUNGHI

Get Funghi has grown organically out of a Swedish/ English love affair between Bengt & Deb and their passion for gathering in the wild. In Sweden, there is a national programme for training people to advise others about which mushrooms are safest for beginners to pick. Bengt completed this course in 2007 and he is therefore a qualified 'svampkonsulent'- mushroom consultant.

With an extensive knowledge of wild mushrooms and a background in the food industry, the couple combine a scrupulous approach to the concept of quality with a genuine enthusiasm for what they do. Their aim is to offer the gourmet food market the very best product in that segment. They proved their credentials by receiving the Golden Fork for Ambient Product of the Year in the Great Taste awards 2015, for their handpicked dried porcini.

www.therarebrandmarket.co.uk/getfunghi

GET FUNGHI DRIED PORCINI MUSHROOMS

PREP: 1 HR   **SERVES:** 6-8

COOK: 1 HR   **PRE HEAT OVEN:** 180C

INGREDIENTS

2 pkts shortcrust pastry
50g cheddar cheese
1 egg, to glaze
Filling:
30g butter
60g onion, minced
1 garlic clove, diced
2 pkts Get Fungi Dried
Porcini Mushrooms,
soaked for 30mins
450g button mushrooms,

sliced
2 tsp coarse salt
1/2 tsp black pepper
2 free range eggs
300ml double cream
30g flour
1 tbsp mixed fresh herbs
(rosemary, thyme, and
sage)
50g cheddar cheese,
grated

METHOD

The amount of pastry depends on the serving dish size. To make the pastry cheesy, roll half of it out to a large rectangle and then sprinkle with the cheese, fold the pastry over and cut in half. Place the other half in the fridge. Grease a 20cm loose-bottomed pie dish and roll out the rest of the pastry to about double the size of the dish, this will incorporate the cheese, then carefully lift it into place, pressing it into the corners, and mend any little rips.

Heat the butter in shallow pan over medium heat. Add the onion and cook until translucent. Add the garlic, cook for 1 minute. Drain the porcini mushroom and keep the liquid. Add the porcini and button mushrooms to pan stirring frequently. Season with salt and pepper.

In large bowl, whisk together the cream, eggs, and flour. Add the mushroom mixture, herbs, and cheese stirring to combine. Pour into the pie base.

Roll out the rest of the pastry in the fridge to the size of the serving dish, then lift on top, pinch together the edges to seal. Brush with the egg wash, poke a couple of holes in the top for steam. Bake for about 45 minutes and the top is golden. Allow to cool.

ARGANIC

Since Arganic launched in 2012, its founder Dana Elemara has grown the business in an organic way. She set out to be the best not the biggest: to supply a product that benefits the customers' health, a livelihood to 600 Berber women and the preservation of a UNESCO protected tree.

From their London base, Arganic work directly with farmer Sidi Yassine in a beautiful village in the south west of Morocco to produce fully traceable, organic argan oil. The oil comes from cold-pressing the seed of the argan fruit. The process of collection and extraction involves several stages, and skilled hand work. It takes 15 hours and 30kg of fruit to produce just one litre - each bottle can be traced back to the tree it came from. The Telegraph newspaper credited this small company with bringing argan oil to the attention of the UK public, as well as some of the best chefs in the world.

www.therarebrandmarket.co.uk/myarganic

ARGANIC ARGAN OIL

PREP: UNDER 30 MINS   **SERVES:** 4-6

COOK: 30 MINS   **PRE HEAT OVEN:** 200C

INGREDIENTS

900g baby spinach leaves
1 large sweet potato, chopped into pieces
1 1/2 tins chickpeas
120g almonds, chopped
60g dried cranberries
140g goat milk cheese, crumbled
1 tbsp Arganic Argan oil

Chickpea Marinade:
2 tbsp soy sauce
2 tsp honey

2 tsp cinnamon
2 tsp paprika
2 tsp cumin
2 tbsp argan oil
juice of 1/2 lemon
pinch of black pepper

Lemon Vinaigrette:
juice of 1/2 lemon
3 tbsp red wine vinegar
2 tbsp argan oil
salt and pepper

METHOD

Scatter sweet potatoes on a baking sheet, toss with oil and season. Roast for 30 minutes.

In a bowl, combine all of the marinade ingredients and whisk. Add the chickpeas and toss to combine.

Whisk together the vinaigrette ingredients in a jug.

To assemble use a large serving plate. Place a bed of spinach, then layer on the warm sweet potatoes and chickpeas, sprinkle the almonds, cranberries and goat milk cheese over the top.

Dress with vinaigrette just before serving.

YOSSI FOODS

Powerful, distinctive flavours and fresh ingredients are the main characteristics of most types of street and fast food in the Middle East. The region celebrates a magical culinary complexity which, for centuries, has been a magnet for individuals, nations and religions alike.

Driven by a passion for healthy, fabulous tasting food, and at the behest of friends who love his cooking Yossi Foods was born. The recipes have been passed down through generations of Yossi's family as they migrated across the Middle East. He makes all his products by hand, with the same care and attention he uses when cooking for family and friends. Each jar of Yossi's condiments is packed with only fresh, natural ingredients that offer incredible versatility and great flavour - no preservatives just a sassy, natural flavour of pickled lemons and spicy chillies guaranteed to liven up any dish.

www.therarebrandmarket.co.uk/yossifoods

YOSSI FOODS PICKLED LEMON SPREAD

PREP: UNDER 30 MINS   **SERVES:** 2

COOK: 15 MINS   **PRE HEAT OVEN:** 180C

INGREDIENTS

200g coley, or any white fish

½ lemon, juiced

1 tbsp Yossi Lemon Spread

2 tbsp organic natural yoghurt

1 chilli, de-seeded and chopped

bunch of coriander

2 garlic cloves, roughly chopped

100g pak choi

METHOD

Place the fish in a non-metallic dish, sprinkle with the lemon juice. Cover and refrigerate for 15-20 minutes.

Using a pestle and mortar, or blender, make a paste with the coriander, chilli and garlic. Add the Yossi lemon spread and yoghurt and mix together.

Coat the fish on both sides with the paste. Place the fish in the middle of a large square of foil. Fold into a loose parcel, turn over the top to seal. Chill in the fridge for at least an hour.

Place the sealed fish parcel on a tray and bake in the oven for about 15 mins, or until the fish is cooked. Steam pak choi for 2 mins or so depending on preferred crunch.

Serve immediately with the pak choi and extra lemon spread.

MARA SEAWEED

Mara, was founded by Fiona Houston and Xa Milne who met at their kids' school playground, and got chatting about foraging and Scotland's natural larder. They became experts in native seaweeds and how to cook them, "All of the 3000 or so species of seaweed are edible, but only some taste good," explains Milne.

Rory MacPhee, Mara's seaweed harvester, wades knee-deep in the coldest, cleanest Scottish waters to pick Kombu and Dulse, and scrambles along rocks to collect precious Pepper Dulse. Ethical, environmentally friendly 'like pruning bushes' and following the crofting tradition, harvesting is seasonal at the lowest monthly tides, during the new and full moon. The crop is hung up to air dry in the and wind, then the seaweed is ground down to capture its intense flavours, freshness and nutritional benefits.

"This superfood was a staple for coastal Scots from prehistoric times. Seaweed is the most highly mineralised vegetable on earth," says Houston. "This is a product to enjoy. We don't want to sell a boring health product taken as pills."

www.therarebrandmarket.co.uk/maraseaweed

mara
SEAWEED
FLAVOURS OF SCOTLAND

Salmon supplied by www.keenanseafood.com

MARA SEAWEED DULSE FLAKES

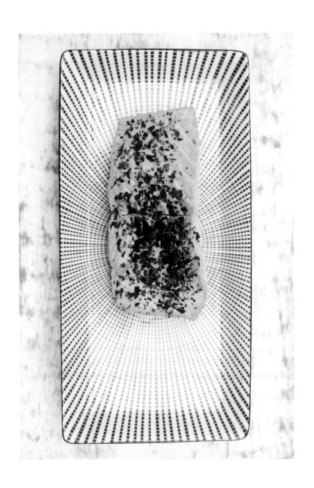

PREP: UNDER 15 MINS **SERVES:** 2

COOK: UNDER 15 MINS

INGREDIENTS

1 litre vegetable stock
2 tbsp miso paste
2 shallots, thinly
sliced diagonally
2 spring onions sliced
2 tsp finely grated
fresh ginger
2 tbsp soy sauce
2x200g pkts udon
noodles
1 tbsp coldpressed

rapeseed oil
2 x 400g skinless
salmon fillets,
2 tbsp sesame seeds
1 tin Mara Seaweed
Dulse Flakes
wasabi paste and
pickled ginger to
serve

METHOD

Pour the stock and miso paste in a saucepan. Bring to the boil. Add the shallots, ginger and soy sauce. Reduce heat and simmer for 5 minutes developing the flavours into a soup. Cook the noodles as per the instructions on the packet.

Mix 2 tablespoons of dulse seaweed flakes with the sesame seeds. Roll and coat the salmon fillets in the mixture.

Heat oil in a non-stick frying pan over high heat. Cook salmon for 2 minutes each side or until almost cooked through. Set aside to cool slightly. Slice salmon.

Divide noodles and soup among serving bowls. Top with salmon, spring onions, more dulse seaweed flakes and serve with the wasabi and pickled ginger.

COBBLE LANE CURED

Adam Brudnowski, Matt Hill and Matt Atkinson met while working at Jamie Oliver's Barbecoa Butcher's shop, where they decided they wanted to go into business together to produce a top-quality, high-welfare British meat product, centered around Brudnowski's skills is charcuterie.

Cobble Lane Cured have a core range of ten products making use of every scrap of meat. Employing a whole range of processes and preparations, they transform these great raw products into delicious hams, salamis, whole cuts, sausages and bacon. They produce in small batches and do not hurry the process at all, or use any chemicals to accelerate, stabilise or artificially enhance the products.

Bringing this altogether has enabled them to create outstanding products - like air-dried hams made from rare breed pigs, moist beef bresaola and traditional smoked pepperoni with ox-heart and pork belly. A fine way to show off the quality of great British meat.
www.therarebrandmarket.co.uk/ cobblelanecured

Cobble Lane
CURED

FENNEL AND GARLIC SALAMI COBBLE LANE CURED

PREP: UNDER 30 MINS   **SERVES:** 6

COOK: UNDER 1 HR   **PRE HEAT OVEN:** 190C

INGREDIENTS

2 tsp argan oil

500g courgette, coarsely grated

4 spring onions, finely chopped

salt

250g white long grain rice

150g goat milk cheese, coarsely grated

2 tbsp chopped mint

1 pkt shortcrust pastry

12 slices Fennel and Garlic Cobble Lane Cured Salami

4 hard-boiled eggs, halved

1 egg, lightly beaten

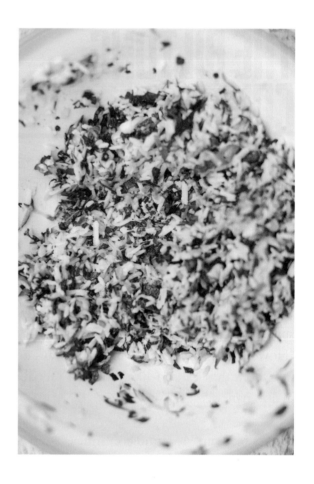

METHOD

Cook the rice as per the packet instructions.

Heat oil in a frying pan over medium heat. Add courgette, spring onion and ½ teaspoon salt. Cook for 3 minutes or until courgette is slightly wilted. Transfer to a bowl and cool, then drain off any excess liquid.

Add cooked rice, goat milk cheese and mint to courgette mixture. Stir to combine and season.

On a baking tray, lightly flour your baking parchment and roll pastry to 25 x 35cm rectangle and cut in half lengthways. Place six slices of salami, slightly overlapping, down the middle of the pastry. Top with half the courgette mix, the egg halves, remaining courgette mix and the last six salami slices.

Put a rectangle of pastry on top and pinch the edges to seal. Brush with egg and bake 30-35 minutes or until pastry is golden. Serve warm or cold.

THE BILTONG COMPANY

South African founders of The Biltong Company, Simon and Monique, live in the UK on the glorious Sussex South Coast. They have been making Biltong for over 25 years.

"We cycle down to the beautiful West Wittering beach, sit on the sand, drink beer and treat ourselves to my latest batch of wet fatty Biltong… my favourite! Always spicy!" says Simon a self-confessed cycling fanatic. "However, Monique is a pain and always demands dry, non fatty, thin-as-you-like, biltong! Talk about high maintenance!"

Pilates teacher Monique continues. "I am always on the go and I really need to up my protein intake. Biltong is the perfect source of low fat protein. The beef used to make the biltong is sourced from Natural Farms Limited and The West Oxfordshire Meat Company. They only use the silverside of the beef to make their products.

"Here at The Biltong Company we have a commitment to quality. We believe in the highest standards for ourselves and for our products. That is why all the spices used, right down to the salt, are organic and sourced from EHL Finest Natural Ingredients and we only use distilled spirit vinegar from Good Food Wines Limited. The very best money can buy for us and for you!" says Simon. "No sugar, no preservatives, no msg, no e-numbers, no gluten."

www.therarebrandmarket.co.uk/ biltongcompany

BILTONG COMPANY

THE CHICHESTER BILTONG COMPANY PERI PERI BILTONG

PREP: UNDER 15 MINS   **SERVES:** 6

INGREDIENTS

Salad dressing:
60ml honey
1 orange, juiced
1/2 lemon, juiced
1 tbsp argan oil
salt and freshly
ground black pepper,
to taste
2 tbsp fresh mint,
chopped

Salad:
1 red grapefruit,
peeled and sliced
1 pink grapefruit,
peeled and sliced
2 clementines, peeled
and sliced
2 oranges, peeled and
sliced
150g Chichester Peri
Peri Biltong, roughly
chopped
salt flakes, to serve
small handful fresh
mint, to serve

METHOD

For the dressing, in a food processor, blitz together the honey and citrus juices and, while the motor is running, add the oil in a slow, steady stream until mixed through. Remove from blender, season and stir in the mint.

For the salad, arrange the fruit on a platter, top with the biltong and season with salt flakes, drizzle with the dressing and scatter over the fresh mint.

QNOLA®

Qnola is a range of truly healthy breakfast products. At Qnola our aim is to make it easier to not only wake up, but to WAKE UP WELL!

Qnola products are made without refined sugar and are paleo, vegan, vegetarian, wheat, gluten, dairy and grain free!

www.qnola.co.uk

Suppers...

IN THIS SECTION YOU WILL FIND TEN SUPPERS PERFECT FOR A RELAXED KITCHEN TABLE MEAL, OR SUITABLE FOR A MORE FORMAL DINNER.

Radishes

LAVINTON LAMB

Shepherdess, Sophie Arlott produces delicious grass-fed lamb from native British breeds such as Hebridean and Southdown, chosen for their excellent texture and flavour. They graze on the rich pastureland of her small Lincolnshire farm. At a time when the origins of food are increasingly important, Arlott takes traceability to its extreme. "It's been called 'hyper-provenance'," she explains. "I'm involved in each stage of the sheep's lives and know every single lamb." But she doesn't farm this way because it is fashionable, she does it because she believes it produces better results - "A happy sheep is a tasty sheep."

The success of Lavinton Lamb is proved not only by her Great Taste awards in 2015 for Southdown lamb, Merguez lamb sausages and Moroccan lamb sausages - but also by the fact that Lavinton Lamb is stocked in no less than six Michelin-starred restaurants.

www.therarebrandmarket.co.uk/lavinton

Image courtesy of Country Living by Brent Darby

LAVINTON

LAVINTON SPRING SHOULDER OF LAMB

PREP: 30 MINS   **SERVES:** 6

COOK: 2 HRS   **PRE HEAT OVEN:** 180C

INGREDIENTS

4 sprigs oregano

4 sprigs thyme

2 sprigs rosemary

2 bay leaves

2 tbsp cold pressed rapeseed oil

1kg spring lamb shoulder on the bone

salt and freshly ground black pepper

8 shallots, peeled

4 garlic cloves, peeled, thinly sliced

2 tbsp balsamic vinegar

225ml dry red wine

1400ml chicken stock

185g semi-pearled farro, rinsed

800g baby turnips, trimmed, scrubbed, halved if large

1 bunch asparagus, trimmed, cut on diagonal into 30cm pieces

370g fresh or frozen peas cooked

METHOD

Tie oregano, thyme, rosemary, and bay leaves with kitchen twine. Heat 1 tablespoon oil in a large, oven-proof casserole over medium-high. Season lamb and seal in pan on all sides. Once sealed remove from the pan. To the same pan, add shallots until browned. Stir in garlic and cook 30 seconds before adding the vinegar. Cook for one minute scraping up browned bits, until syrupy.

Add wine, bring to a boil, and cook until reduced by about a quarter. Add the stock, lamb, and herb bundle. Bring to a boil, reduce heat, and place in the oven for 1 hour and 20 mins.

Remove from the oven and put back on hob on a low heat. Stir in the farro and turnips and cook for 15 to 20 minutes. Blanch the asparagus and peas.

Remove the lamb from the heat. Add asparagus and peas to the lamb. Season and serve with a drizzle of oil.

PUCKETT'S PICKLES

Puckett's Pickles are wholesomely natural, gloriously colourful and joyfully British. No nasty preservatives, no needless food miles - just seasonal produce, bright fresh herbs and rich whole spices (and a secret soupçon of Granny's know-how). Nothing tickles the taste buds like a Puckett's Pickle. "As a child my most favourite meals were what my Mother used to call 'fridge cleaners,' enthuses Sarah Puckett. "Left over meats; cheese; bread; bubble and squeak - Mother would chuck in anything! Plus of course, my Father's amazing chutneys and pickles. The table would be laden full of goodies, the atmosphere was relaxed and the conversation flowed as we grazed - just heaven".

Puckett's Pickles' customers get that same warm feeling when they see a homemade jar on the table, confident their taste buds are about to be tickled.

www.therarebrandmarket.co.uk/ puckettspickles

151

PORK BELLY WITH SWEET AND SOUR SLAW

PUCKETT'S PICKLES

PREP: UNDER 30 MINS   **SERVES:** 4-6

COOK: 2 HRS   **PRE HEAT OVEN:** 200C

INGREDIENTS

1 kg pork belly from
Red Hill Farm
salt & pepper
50g seaweed strips
40g ginger peeled and
cut into thin strips
3 medium carrots,
grated
250g mango peeled,
cut into strips
100g peanuts

juice of half a lime
handful of coriander
chopped
handful of mint
shredded
1tbsp Puckett's Pickles
Cucumber and Lemon,
finely sliced
1 tbsp caster sugar
80ml rice wine vinegar
1 tbsp groundnut oil

METHOD

Firstly pat the pork belly skin dry and then score
and season it thoroughly. Place pork in oven for 45
minutes. Then reduce temperature to 180c and cook
for one hour.

Meanwhile finely chop the Puckett's Pickles
Cucumber and Lemon along with the mango, mint,
ginger, seaweed strips and coriander and mix with the
grated carrot. Add the peanuts, the juice of at least
half a lime, some caster sugar and the vinegar and oil
and combine thoroughly. Place in the fridge to cool.

Remove the belly from the oven and slice into strips,
serve with a large spoonful of the cucumber and
carrot salad on the side.

BARONSCOURT ESTATE

Baronscourt Estate is the home of Ireland's finest wild venison, situated in the foothills of the famous Sperrin Mountains in County Tyrone. The herd of Japanese Sika deer were initially introduced into a deer park in 1751, but since 1920 they have existed wild on the Estate. Baronscourt Sika deer thrive in the forests and woodlands on the Estate's natural and nourishing flora and fauna. Throughout the year they feed on succulent myrtle bog, ryegrass and tasty saplings which are naturally free of any additives or growth promoters.

Baronscourt wild venison is a sustainable source of meat; an annual deer count is arranged each year by trained stalkers who assess the population and its general health. A selective cull takes place in order to balance the breeding population, with the likely food source for the season. The Estate's detailed management of this herd was recognised when it received the Laurent Perrier Award for Wild Game Conservation. Sika is a very lean and succulent meat, having the lowest calories and cholesterol levels compared to any other red meat products. Combined with the high levels of protein, venison can be classified as a red meat 'super food.'
www.therarebrandmarket.co.uk/baronscourt

WILD SIKA VENISON

PREP: UNDER 15 MINS   **SERVES:** 2

COOK: UNDER 15 MINS

INGREDIENTS

3 tbsp cold pressed
rapeseed oil
220g Baronscourt Sika
Venison per person
salt and ground
pepper
handful parsley
chopped

1 medium onion,
halved and thinly
sliced
1½ tbsp
Worcestershire sauce
1 tbsp butter

METHOD

Heat one tablespoon of oil in large, heavy bottom pan.
Season the venison, cook until dark brown and crusty,
3 to 5 minutes per side for medium-rare dependent
on thickness.

Remove from the pan and set aside. While the venison
rests, heat remaining oil on medium heat. Add onion
and cook until tender, then add Worcestershire sauce
and butter.

Plate up the steak thinly sliced and top with the onion
sauce and some chopped parsley.

Serving suggestion: serve with sprouting brocolli,
cook the broccoli in a steamer for approx 6-8 minutes
or until just tender.

APPLE COUNTY CIDER

Great cider represents a timeless joy to Ben and
Steph Culpin from Apple County Cider. They make
real cider and perry from their orchards in the lush,
rolling Monmouthshire hills. Their approach to cider-
making is reverential, akin to winemaking. Each cider
is made from 100% freshly pressed juice from single,
bitter-sweet apple varieties such as Dabinett, Michelin,
Vilberie, Brown Snout and Yarlington Mill. The juice sits
in the barn and enjoys a slow, long cold fermentation
throughout the winter months. Here the ciders develop
their distinguished character and complex flavours.
In the spring the vats are 'racked off' for a secondary
fermentation. The cider is ready to enjoy in early
summer. Apple County is putting Monmouthshire
and indeed Wales, back on the map for cider making.
Discover a taste of Apple County for yourself by visiting
the farm, or by simply opening a bottle.

**www.therarebrandmarket.co.uk/
applecountycider**

CIDER BRAISED CHICKEN

APPLE COUNTY CIDER VILBERIE MEDIUM DRY CIDER

PREP: UNDER 30 MINS **SERVES:** 6-8

COOK: UNDER 45 MINS **PRE HEAT OVEN:** 175C

INGREDIENTS

8 chicken thighs (bone in, skin on)
salt and ground black pepper
2 tbsp olive oil
1 large onion, peeled, cut into slices
4 garlic cloves, diced
250ml Apple County Cider Vilberie

medium dry
115ml chicken stock
1 tbsp stoneground mustard
80ml organic double cream
750g dessert apples, peeled, cored and roughly chopped

METHOD

Rinse chicken, pat dry and lightly season. In a large oven-proof casserole dish heat half the olive oil and brown the chicken thighs skin-side down in the pan. Cook for five minutes on each side. Remove chicken from the pan and set aside.

Add remainder of olive oil to the pan and on a gentle heat cook the onion and garlic until onions are softened. Raise heat back to medium and add the Vilberie cider and chicken stock. Scrape the bottom of the pan and then boil for a minute. Add the mustard, double cream and the apples.

Return the chicken thighs to the pan, cover and place into the oven. Cook for 35 minutes or until chicken is cooked.

Scoop the chicken and sauce into bowls and serve with crusty loaf of bread for mopping up the onion and apple sauce.

THREE CENTS CO.

Three Cents are the first premium Greek beverages made entirely from natural ingredients without any added preservatives or artificial flavouring. The idea behind the brand comes from the great depression era in the United States of America. During the prohibition, when alcohol was banned, bars were closed and the soda shops filled the social void. Soda water was the cheapest beverage that someone could buy at two cents a glass. People used to order it as a two cents plain and if they asked for a syrup to add a flavour they had to pay one more cent: total three cents. Three Cents the brand was created by three bartenders, Dimitris Dafopoulos, George Bagos, George Tsirikos and the owner of importing distributing company Granikal, Vassilis Kalantzis. The product range consists of six beverages: Two Cents Plain, Tonic Water, Lemon Tonic, Pink Grapefruit Soda, Ginger Beer and Mediterranean Tonic.
www.therarebrandmarket.co.uk/threecents

Seabass supplied by www.keenanseafood.com

THREE CENTS CO. LEMON TONIC

PREP: UNDER 30 MINS   **SERVES:** 4

COOK: UNDER 15 MINS   **PRE HEAT OVEN:**

INGREDIENTS

4 x 200g sea bass fish filet
rapeseed oil for frying
chilli jam
Chapati:
360g strong wholemeal
flour
pinch salt
1 tsp each cumin, garlic
powder and mustard
seeds
1/4 tsp crushed chilli
120g cooked lentils
water to form a firm
dough - start with 115ml

Batter:
120g flour
2 tsp baking powder
pinch salt
225ml Three Cents Co.
Lemon Tonic Water
Salad:
bunch of coriander,
chopped
1 cucumber, chopped
1 pepper, chopped
1 kohlrabi, grated

METHOD

Combine chapati ingredients forming a firm dough that is moist but not sticky. Let rest for 10 minutes covered with an inverted bowl.

Divide into 8 pieces and roll out on a lightly floured surface.

Heat a dry frying pan before adding the chapati. Let it slightly puff and turn once. Remove from the heat.

For the batter, beat all the ingredients together, dip the fish in and fry over a high heat until fish has cooked through.

Mix up all the salad ingredients and divide over the chapatis, top with fish and a side bowl of chilli jam for dipping.

COALTOWN COFFEE

This modest operation is only a year old, but Coaltown is part of a new breed of coffee entrepreneurs who are giving caffeine worshippers an alternative to the bland, generic brands served at commercial chains.

Founded by Gordon James and his son Scott, Coaltown Coffee is a craft, speciality roastery based at the foothills of the Black Mountains in Wales. "The art of roasting is how you control the rise in temperature," says James Senior.

Based in the garage at James' house, he hand roasts, small 12kg batches on the Probatone 12 roaster. "The beans cooking inside are about to hit a toasty 225C," he adds. Within moments the sweet smell of freshly roasted Arabica fill the air. They roast weekly for optimum freshness. Recognised for its dedication to quality, Coaltown has been awarded a Great Taste award for its espresso blend Pit Prop No1 and No2.

However important the flavour is, and it is parmount, Coaltown Coffee are ethically responsible too. "Our coffee hunters only source green coffee beans directly from small farms across the world that are working in line with International Labour Laws," explains James. "We pay a high price for our beans to ensure everyone benefits, from the coffee farmer to the picker, this is called relationship coffee."
www.therarebrandmarket.co.uk/ coaltowncoffee

COALTOWN
COFFEE ROASTERS

COALTOWN COFFEE ESTATE ESPRESSO BLEND

PREP: 30 MINS   **SERVES:** 2-4

COOK: 1.5 HRS   **PRE HEAT OVEN:** 180C

INGREDIENTS

1 tbsp ground cumin
2 tbsp freshly ground
Coaltown Coffee
Estate Espresso Blend
salt and freshly
ground pepper
1 tbsp chilli powder
1/8 tsp cayenne
pepper

1/2 tsp ground
cinnamon
1kg Tomahawk steak
from Higher Hacknall
vegetable oil
1/2 kg potatoes
peeled and cut into
chips

METHOD

In a small bowl, combine the spices and the coffee.
Pat meat dry, rub lightly with vegetable oil and then
rub the seasoning into the meat. Put on a plate and
refrigerate.

Par boil the potatoes, then leave them to cool before
deep frying to crisp and golden brown.

Preheat a griddle to high. Drizzle both sides of the
steak with oil, then grill, about 5 minutes per side to
seal. Transfer to a baking tray and place in the oven
for an hour and 10 minutes. Let rest for 10 minutes
before slicing and serving with hot chips.

This wonderful coffee based spicy rub can be used on
any cut of beef: left to marinade the flavours develop
beautifully.

BENNETT & DUNN

Bennett & Dunn cold pressed rapeseed oil is produced by husband and wife team Rupert and Tracey Bennett. Rupert, who has 30 years experience farming in Shropshire, takes great pride in producing a superior quality product. The rapeseed is cold pressed, triple filtered and then hand-bottled by Rupert on the farm. The oil is GM free, gluten free and the production process is chemical free, ensuring the rapeseed oil retains all of its health benefits and delicious flavour.

It has a gentle creamy, nutty flavour and is a healthy alternative to olive oil for marinades, dipping and drizzling. It also cooks at a higher temperature without effecting its many health benefits, character or taste. Unlike olive oil, rapeseed oil is also ideal for roasting, baking and stir-fries, and can be used for family cooking at every mealtime.

**www.therarebrandmarket.co.uk/
bennettanddunn**

Salmon supplied by www.keenanseafood.com

OIL INFUSED SALMON

BENNETT & DUNN COLD PRESSED RAPESEED OIL

PREP: UNDER 15 MINS   **SERVES:** 4

COOK: UNDER 30 MINS

INGREDIENTS

4 x 150-160g portions of salmon boned and skinned

250-300ml Bennett & Dunn cold pressed rapeseed oil

1tsp fennel seeds

couple of sprigs of thyme

10 black peppercorns

1tsp flaky sea salt

8 or so spears of asparagus

handful of wild garlic leaves, washed

METHOD

Heat the oil in a saucepan which is large enough to hold all the salmon fillets. Add the fennel seeds, thyme, peppercorns and salt. Leave to infuse, cover and cook over a low heat for 4-5 minutes. Add the salmon fillets, cover with a lid and remove from the heat.

Cook the asparagus separately in boiling, salted water until tender, then drain. Cut the asparagus into three diagonal pieces. Place in a saucepan with two tablespoons of cooking oil and the wild garlic leaves.

Season and heat for a minute, stirring until the leaves are just starting to wilt.

Pop the vegetables on to warm serving plates and top each one with a piece of salmon and a sprinkling of thyme.

168

COEDCANLAS

Coedcanlas lies in the far west of Wales, in the heart of Pembrokeshire. Remote and unspoilt, Coedcanlas provides a perfect setting for Nick and Annette Tonkin to gather and create a unique range, of artisan products. From a wooden shed on the eastern shore of the Daugleddau Estuary, Nick nurtures his bees in 90 wooden hives. Using the family's traditional beekeeping and breeding methods, he has spent years developing naturally strong and healthy bees. The honey is gathered from a multitude of Pembrokeshire's wild flowers: bluebells, dandelions, may, blackberries and wild clover. It is full of delicate and aromatic flavours that Nick goes to great lengths to preserve. Filtered using only gravity and time, the goal is for the cunsumer to taste the honey exactly as the bees left it in the comb. Delicious, unadulterated and pure.

www.therarebrandmarket.co.uk/coedcanlas

COEDCANLAS

HONEY GLAZED PORK FILLET AND RHUBARB

COEDCANLAS WILD LEMON BLOSSOM HONEY

PREP: UNDER 15 MINS   **SERVES:** 2

COOK: UNDER 1 HR   **PRE HEAT OVEN:** 170C

INGREDIENTS

1tbsp olive oil
400g pork fillet
1 sprig rosemary
125g rhubarb, cut into 4cm lengths
100ml water
2-3 tbsp Coedcanlas Wild Lemon
Blossom Honey

METHOD

To begin, place the oil in the roasting pan and put in the oven to heat for at least 3 minutes. Then place the pork into the hot oil and roll it about lightly to seal the juices in. Add rosemary to the pork and return to oven for 20 minutes.

After this time remove and turn the pork over, returning it to the oven for another 10 minutes. Whilst the pork is in the oven, cut up the rhubarb and then add it to the roasting pan with the water and honey and cook for a further 10 minutes.

Check to make sure the pork is cooked and then remove the roasting pan from the oven and leave to rest for 5 minutes before serving.

Carve the pork into slices and spoon over the soft honey rhubarb and juices. This can be served with some beautiful steamed vegetables of your choice.

HIGHER HACKNELL FARM

In 1985, Tim and Jo Buddon came to Higher Hacknell Farm in South Devon, with a determination to farm in a way that worked with nature and not against it. So, in 1988 they started farming organically, a system which they believe offers many common-sense answers to the problems facing agriculture, the food industry and the environment. Organic standards embrace all aspects of the farming system, most especially animal welfare, wildlife conservation and food safety. Higher Hacknell Farm produces the finest organic meat. When you buy direct from the family farm and butchery, you can guarantee the true provenance of organic meat raised to the highest welfare standards. The Buddons enjoy producing their own food: vegetables from the garden, cider from the orchard and meat from their own animals. It progressed as a natural part of farming life - from feeding their own family in the beginning to delivering produce to homes nationwide.

www.therarebrandmarket.co.uk/higherhacknell

HIGHER HACKNELL LAMB LOIN

PREP: UNDER 30 MINS **SERVES:** 4 - 6

COOK: OVER 1 HOUR **PRE HEAT OVEN:** 150C

INGREDIENTS

2x 500g Higher Hacknell Lamb Loin sliced into medallions
2 bay leaves
splash of white wine
1 small bunch parsley plus a little more chopped for garnish
1 ½ tsp salt
1 tbsp rapeseed oil
1 small turnip, diced
4-6 small carrots, chopped
4-6 small onions, roughly chopped
10-12 broad bean pods, shelled and skinned
10-12 pea pods, shelled or 2 handfuls frozen
2 good handfuls lettuce shredded - little gem, oak leaf

METHOD

Heat the oil in a small heavy-based pan and thoroughly brown the pieces of lamb. Tranfer the medallions to a large pot, tip off any fat and deglaze the pan with the white wine. Tip the deglazed juices into the saucepan containing the lamb then cover with water. Add the salt, bay leaves and parsley. Bring to the boil, cover, leave on a very low heat and poach for approx 1 hour until the meat is tender. Add in the onion, carrots and turnips, and then simmer for ten minutes. Finally add the peas, broad beans and lettuce. Warm through for a further three minutes. If the lamb has already poached remove from the stock and leave to rest, adding it back when all the vegetables are done. Place one or two medallions into each bowl, pour over some stock and garnish with chopped parsley.

PALFREY AND HALL

Experienced butchers Shaun Palfrey and Deaglan Hall are a team of two. They are passionate about traditional butchery and supplying local meat. They specialise in bespoke cutting, curing and smoking for private customers, smallholders and caterers.

"With 25 years of local butchery experience between us, we can safely say that we know our meat," says Hall. "In 2013, we decided to go into partnership together, and set up Palfrey & Hall to provide an artisan service for the meat loving community. Our emphasis is on local meats and the craft of butchery. Our Suffolk black bacon is a good exmple: cured using Sir Roger Porter's ale from the renowned local brewery at Earl Soham, which we mix with molasses and black treacle. The result is a distinctively dark, rich and sweet taste, which perfectly counterbalances the flavours in the salted pork."

Palfrey and Hall know the provenance of all of the meat which passes through their butchers. "We might even be able to point out the field it was raised in," says Hall. "We take time to source the best quality meats - pork, chicken, lamb, beef, venison, even water buffalo and goat."

www.therarebrandmarket.co.uk/palfreyandhall

PALFREY & HALL

PURVEYORS OF **THE FINEST QUALITY** LOCAL MEATS

ESTABLISHED 2013

COD, HAM AND CAPERS

PALFREY AND HALL WILTSHIRE STYLE SMOKED HAM

PREP: UNDER 15 MINS **SERVES:** 2

COOK: UNDER 15 MINS **PRE HEAT OVEN:** 180C

INGREDIENTS

2 x 400g fresh cod
300g Palfrey and Hall Wiltshire Smoked Ham, diced
4 shallots, finely chopped
2 tsp capers
2 large handfuls of parsley, chopped
1-2 lemon, juiced
4 tbsp rapeseed oil
1 tbsp flour, seasoned

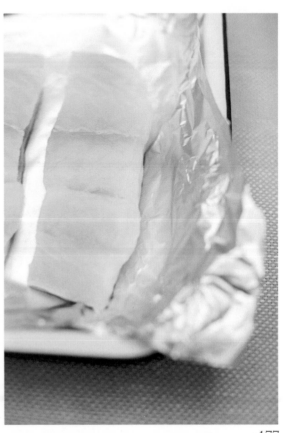

METHOD

In a pan add one tablespoon of oil, add the shallots and cook until soft. Remove from the heat. When cool add the capers, parsley and a squeeze of lemon juice.

In an oven-proof frying pan, heat a second tablespoon of oil. Lightly dust the cod fillet in flour and pan sear until golden brown. Pop into the oven for four minutes.

Flash fry the ham in the last of the oil.

To serve plate up the cod, sprinkle with the ham and pile on the confit shallot mix.

EST 2014 — LONDON

SWEET VIRTUES

Superfood Alchemy

great taste 2015

At Sweet Virtues we believe eating should be an entirely healthy and indulgent experience. All products are made with organic ingredients.

Our range is true guilt- free snacking and exquisite packaging, so the perfect gift.

www.sweetvirtues.co.uk

Desserts...

IN THIS SECTION YOU WILL FIND
TEN SCRUMPTIOUS DESSERTS
WHICH ARE SURE TO DELIGHT THIS
SPRING AND SUMMER!

Blood Orange

SAVEUR DU MAROC

Orange blossom water frames many of life's special moments in Morocco; from hands sprinkled with orange blossom water prior to serving mint tea, to fountains filled with orange blossom at traditional weddings. The flowers used in Saveur Du Maroc's Orange Blossom Water are selected from the finest bitter orange trees in the groves surrounding the city of Marrakech, then lovingly hand-crafted by a local artisan producer. This floral water is prepared by steeping orange blossom heads in fresh spring water, and draws on a traditional steam distillation method, which ensures the pure aroma is captured naturally and beautifully. After dinner, a traditional Middle Eastern café blanc is simply created by adding a splash of orange blossom water to a steaming cup of hot water. A much-loved Moroccan dessert combines thin slices of sweet oranges, soaked in orange blossom water, with a sprinkle of cinnamon and light drizzle of honey.

**www.therarebrandmarket.co.uk/
saveurdumaroc**

SAVEUR DU MAROC ORANGE BLOSSOM

PREP: UNDER 30 MINS   **SERVES:** 12 - 16

COOK: 1.5 HRS   **PRE HEAT OVEN:** 200C

INGREDIENTS

350g caster sugar
6 x free range egg whites
1 1/2 tsp of Saeur Du Maroc
Orange Blossom Water
big handful of pistachio nuts,
finely chopped

METHOD

In an ovenproof dish, warm sugar for 5 mins in the oven. Turn the oven temperature down to 105C.

Beat the egg whites on high in a mixer until they are stiff. Then slow down the mixer and, whilst still mixing, slowly add the sugar. When mixed together slowly add the orange blossom water.

Line a baking tray with parchment paper.

Carefully spoon the meringue into balls and either dip them into the chopped pistachios, or, if you find it easier sprinkle the nuts onto the individual meringues, after they have been placed on the paper. Cook in the oven for an hour, turn off the heat and leave for another half hour.

Remove and leave to cool. Delicious on their own or served with cream and fruit.

EMILY FRUIT CRISPS

Emily Fruit Crisps make delicious healthy snacks in fabulous packs that have all the goodness of fruit with the crunch of a crisp! There's no funny stuff going on either: no preservatives, no additives, no added sugars, no e-numbers and they are gluten-free too. There's nothing but a little oil and lots of fruity deliciousness. More good news - they have half the fat content of popcorn and have four times less fat than the average fried potato crisp, so are a great way to consume more of your five a day.

Founders, Emily and Alex are partners in life as well as in business. They met in London and fell in love travelling the world together, sharing their passion for all things foodie. Alex, ever the romantic, named the brand after Emily so - as it says on the handwritten note on the back of the packs - "I could see your name wherever I went."
www.therarebrandmarket.co.uk/ emilyfruitcrisps

CRUNCHY NAUGHTY RHUBARB TRIFLE

EMILY FRUIT CRISPS CRUNCHY APPLE

PREP: UNDER 30 MINS   **SERVES:** 4-6

COOK: UNDER 30 MINS

INGREDIENTS

1 x 350g shop bought
Madeira sponge cake
(or make a 20cm sponge
cake)
1 pkt Emily Fruit Crunchy
Apple Crisps
Rhubarb liqueur

Compote:
200g rhubarb, sliced
50g golden caster sugar
100ml water

Topping:
125g rhubarb, chopped
small on the diagonal
200ml boiling water
50g sugar

Cream:
350g thick double cream
1 tbsp sugar
1 lemon, juice and zest
100g Greek yoghurt

METHOD

Make the compote by placing the rhubarb, water and sugar in a pan over a medium heat. Stir occasionally until the sugar has dissolved and the fruit has softened. Remove from the heat and let cool in the fridge.

Whip the cream, sugar, lemon zest and juice together. Then fold in Greek yoghurt. Keep refrigerated until ready to use.

To make the topping, in a heat resistant bowl, pour boiling water over the rhubarb and sugar. Then cover with foil and leave to cool.

To assemble the trifle, add a layer of sponge into your serving bowl, splash in Rhubarb liqueur, then a dollop of cream, some compote and repeat. Then sprinkle the drained, chopped rhubarb and a large handful of Emily Fruit Crisps on top for extra crunch.

JESS'S LADIES ORGANIC FARM MILK

Jess Vaughan's family have been farming at Hardwicke Farm in gorgeous Gloucestershire for three generations. They nurture a small herd of 70 cows - the 'ladies' as they are affectionately known. In the summer the herd graze on lush organic pasture and in winter they feed on organic clover silage harvested in the summer. The family believe, quite simply, that happy, healthy cows make better milk. This natural farming method creates well-being and means many of the 'ladies' are descendents of the original 1955 three-strong herd: Bluebird, Gypsy and Glow-Worm. The dairy products are produced by hand on-site. The milk, cream and luxurious natural yoghurt are as fresh as you can get, never homogenised, simply pasteurised, bottled and on the shelf within hours of leaving the 'ladies.' Super fresh, unhomogenised, processed on-site and produced by these beautiful cows grazing on rich organic pastures, all contributes to the flavour of this award winning produce.

www.therarebrandmarket.co.uk/ theladiesorganicmilk

JESS'S LADIES
ORGANIC
FARM MILK

JESS'S LADIES ORGANIC LUXURIOUS YOGURT

PREP: UNDER 1 HR **SERVES:** 8 - 10

COOK: CHILL OVERNIGHT

INGREDIENTS

250g digestive biscuits
90g unsalted butter
40g toasted almonds
20g gelatin
2 lemons, juice & zest
500g Jess's Ladies Luxury Organic Yogurt
200g honey
250g mascarpone/ cream cheese
75g Jess's Ladies Double or Clotted Cream
A selection of fresh seasonal berries - we used blackberries, raspberries and blueberries.

METHOD

Base: crush the biscuits and almonds to a fine consistency in a food processor. Melt the butter and mix with the biscuit. Press into a 20 cm cake tin and place in the fridge.

Filling: place gelatin and lemon juice in a small heat-proof bowl and set over a small saucepan with simmering water (over low heat). Stir until gelatin is melted, remove from saucepan and set aside. Combine all the remaining filling ingredients in the bowl of a large food processor, and process until well-combined. With the machine running, drizzle the warm lemon/gelatin mixture in and process another 30 seconds - make sure it is mixed in thoroughly or the cheesecake will not set evenly.

To assemble: pour cheesecake mixture into the cooled base. Cover and refrigerate overnight. Decorate with a selection of seasonal fruit.

PUMP STREET BAKERY

Pump Street Bakery was founded five years ago by self-taught baker Chris Brennan and his daughter Joanna. They produce the highest quality sourdough bread and pastries, in the village bakery, a few hundred yards from their Number 1 Pump Street Café. They have an uncompromising standard for ingredients and craftsmanship. The pair have since turned their all-consuming focus to chocolate. They produce handmade single origin chocolate bars in small batches, from beans imported directly to them from family farms around the world. They strive to make the most delicious chocolate possible and that starts with buying the very best cocoa beans. Each bar can be traced back to the single origin of cocoa bean they were made from. The chocolate has won numerous awards in 2015, both within the chocolate industry and at the Great Taste awards.
www.therarebrandmarket.co.uk/ pumpstreetbakery

PUMP STREET BAKERY MADAGASCAR MILK CHOCOLATE

PREP: UNDER 15 MINS   **SERVES:** 4-8 DEPENDING ON POT SIZE

COOK: UNDER 30 MINS

INGREDIENTS

300g Pump Street Bakery Madagascar Milk Chocolate, broken into pieces
75ml milk
112g of sugar
30g corn flour
1tsp vanilla extract
pinch of sea salt
sprinkles of choice
honey

METHOD

Firstly break the chocolate into pieces.

Using a medium sized saucepan, pour in the sugar, salt and corn flour, and mix with a whisk to combine. Then add all the milk, whisking to minimize lumps, finally add the vanilla.

Turn the heat on medium, stirring occasionally. Cook for at least ten minutes as this will fully cook the corn starch taste out. If it comes to a boil that is fine, but do not let it burn - lower the heat to make it a gentle simmer.

After the 10 minutes is up, add the chocolate and stir until it is completely melted. Remove from heat. If there are any lumps pass it through a sieve.

This mixture may either be poured into one big container or several small, individual ones. Cool in the fridge for 2-3 hours. This pudding will keep in the fridge for up to four days - don't forget to cover and most importantly decorate, we used thick honey as 'glue' and dipped the jars in colourful sprinkles.

THE M'HENCHA COMPANY

In 2003, founder of the The M'hencha Company, Sophie Browne was diagnosed with a chronic autoimmune disorder. By the end of 2009 she had made the decision to leave her corporate sales and marketing career to create a sustainable bakery business, whilst making lifestyle changes to improve her health.

Twelve months later with significantly improved health, and one unsustainable business plan under her belt, Sophie hit on the idea of making a unique version of M'hencha - a traditional Moroccan celebration cake. Re-working five recipes from Algeria to Morocco, Sophie hand bakes her M'hencha at her micro bakery in the Cotswolds. This taste journey for the palate has great foodie credentials including a Golden Fork, from the Guild of Fine Food.

www.therarebrandmarket.co.uk/
themhenchacompany

THE
M'HENCHA
COMPANY

ORANGE, CINNAMON & DATE M'HENCHA CAKE

PREP: UNDER 15 MINS   **SERVES:**   8

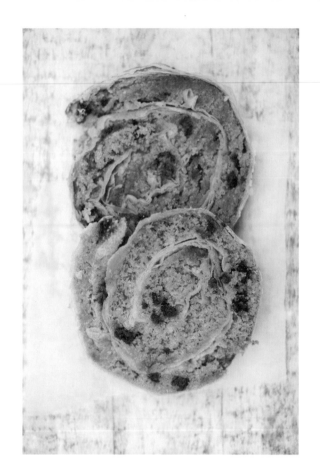

INGREDIENTS

1 M'Hencha Date, Orange and Cinnamon
Cake, cut in half horizontally
450g Jess's Ladies Organic Double Cream
4 cardamom pods
6 egg yolks
2 tsp corn flour
60g golden caster sugar
1 punnet blueberries

METHOD

Dry fry the cardamom pods for about a minute. Then
crush them and put in a saucepan with the cream and
simmer. Remove from the heat and leave for an hour
to allow flavours to infuse.

Separate the eggs. In a large bowl, whisk the yolks,
sugar and corn flour together. Warm the cardamom
cream and whisk it into the mixture: when blended
pass the crème patisserie through a sieve.

When cool spread inside the M'hencha cake and top
with fruit. We used blueberries but almost any fruit
works here.

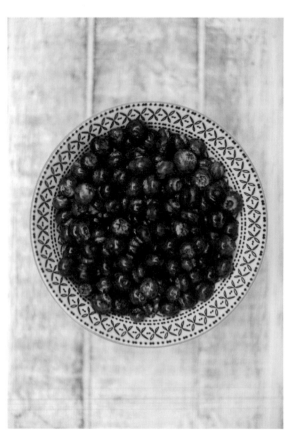

RADNOR PRESERVES

In five short years Joanna Morgan has gone from a cottage with no electricity, a glut of home-grown fruit and veg and her grandfather's preserves recipe book, to winning over 20 international awards. Radnor Preserves uses the finest natural ingredients to provide sublime flavours for the most discerning palate. All hand-prepared and cooked in small batches, the time-honoured tradition of preserve making captures the seasons. The transformation of raw ingredients into incredibly precious jewels creates a real sense of wonder. Radnor Preserves won a Double Gold at the World Marmalade Awards for its savoury Smoky Campfire Marmalade, the highest prize in the world of marmalade. Selfridges then selected Radnor Preserves for its Meet the Maker campaign, introducing undiscovered artisan food producers across the British Isles to its discerning foodie customers. Bentley Motors also chose their products to help launch their new Bentley at the Frankfurt Motor Show, and the Tate Gallery now serves Radnor Preserves on their menu.

www.therarebrandmarket.co.uk/ radnorpreserves

Founder image courtesy of Hermione McCosh

RADNOR PRESERVES

RADNOR PRESERVES MARMALADE

PREP: 1 HR

SERVES: 8

COOK: UNDER 30 MINS

PRE HEAT OVEN: 170C

INGREDIENTS

Pastry:
350g plain flour
225g unsalted butter, cubed
100g icing sugar
pinch of salt
3 free range egg yolks

Filling:
1 jar Radnor Orange Marmalade
1 orange, juiced
100ml water
150g butter, cubed
3 whole eggs
4 egg yolks

METHOD

In a food processor, pulse the flour, butter, icing sugar and salt together. Then add the egg yolks and pulse for a few minutes. Put the pastry onto a floured surface and work it until mixture comes together as a dough. Wrap in cling film and put in the fridge. After at least an hour, roll out the pastry and place into a 25cm tart tin pushing it down and into the sides. Put pastry in the freezer for 10 minutes.

Now line the tart tin with baking parchment and fill with baking beans or dried pulses. Bake for about 15 minutes or until the pastry is firm, then remove the beans and cook for about 5 minutes more, until golden brown and biscuity. Set aside while you make the filling.

Put the orange juice, marmalade, water and butter in a pan and warm through until the butter melts. Whisk the whole eggs with the egg yolks and add them to the pan with the marmalade.

Cook on medium heat for 5 minutes - it will become opaque when it's ready. Quickly pour the mixture into the baked tart shell.

After allowing it to cool for a few minutes, place under a hot grill until you get big black spots on the top but the pastry is not burned.

197

TZEKOS ORGANIC HERBS

The Tzekos Organic Herb Farm spreads across 11,000 square metres on a sunny hillside overlooking Mount Olympus. The mild winters, cool summers and frequent air currents from the nearby sea create the perfect microclimate.

All the herbal plants are local; they can usually be seen growing naturally in Greece and they are well known for their therapeutic and nutritional values, dating back to ancient times. The Tzekos venture began with the search for plants with one simple but critical feature: to be grown from pure local seed varieties. The plants are handpicked at the optimum time for each variety, dried naturally in order to preserve all their natural properties and packed by hand.

www.therarebrandmarket.co.uk/ tzekosorganicherbs

Photograph by Anastasis Stratakis

TZEKOS ORGANIC HERBS

CITRUS AND THYME POSSET

TZEKOS HERBS THYME HERBS

PREP: UNDER 30 MINS   **SERVES:** 4

COOK: UNDER 1 HR   **PRE HEAT OVEN:** 160C

INGREDIENTS

240ml milk
1 lemon, peel
1 teaspoon Tzekos Thyme
1 large egg
1 egg white
115g golden caster sugar
2 lemons, juiced
1 sprig of Tzekos Thyme

METHOD

Place the milk, lemon peel and thyme in a small pan over medium heat. Bring to a low simmer, stirring, until it has reduced by one third. Remove from the heat. Allow to steep for a few minutes.

Whisk the egg, egg white, sugar, and lemon juice together in a small bowl. Strain to remove the lemon peel and thyme. Stir in the milk. Pour into 4 small oven-proof dishes such as ramekins. Place in the baking dish, and pour in boiling water to about 1 inch up the sides of the ramekins. Bake for 50 minutes or until set.

Cool and serve warm, topped with a tiny sprig of thyme.

OOH LA LA ARTISAN CONFECTIONERY

"One of the things I love about the French," says Ooh la la Confectionery owner Karen Schneid, "is how they are unwilling to accept anything but the best."

A lawyer by day and sweet maker by night, Schneid lived her double life for many years before she decided to transform her hobby of French confectionery into a viable business. A self-confessed Francophile, she sourced families in France that had been making sweet delicacies for hundreds of years, so each variety is accompanied by a quaint back story. Legend has it that Queen Marie Antoinette would feast on marshmallows in full view of the public who would beg to taste them, she refused to share, even when implored to do so by Louis XVI. The greedy queen was recorded as saying: "Marshmallows, my dear nation, are mine. As far as the people are concerned, let them eat cake." Thus the French revolution was sparked!

Schneid's success can be attributed to her perfectionism and passion for authenticity. "I always go the extra mile and use only the best and most expensive ingredients - for example my vanilla comes from Madagascar," she explains. To quote the French queen, "There is nothing new except what has been forgotten." Schneid is not reinventing, but rediscovering the lost art of making confections.

www.therarebrandmarket.co.uk/
oohlalaconfectionery

Ooh la la®
ARTISAN CONFECTIONERY

ORANGE AND NOUGAT GELATI

OOH LA LA CONFECTIONERY FRENCH PISTACHIO NOUGAT

PREP: UNDER 30 MINS   **SERVES:** 10

INGREDIENTS

Glace:
450ml double cream
1 orange zest
150g Ooh la la French
Pistachio Nougat,
chopped, extra for
decoration if desired
200g sugar
15 cherries, pitted
and chopped

Cherry coulis:
250g cherries, pitted
and chopped
120ml water
2 tbsp golden caster
sugar
2 lemons, juice

METHOD

Line a 25cm loaf tin with plastic wrap both crosswise and lengthwise, leaving a sling overhang.

Glace: whip the chilled cream to soft peaks and chill in the fridge.

Mix the sugar, orange zest, nougat and cherries together and then add this to the chilled cream.

Scrape the nougat mix into the prepared loaf tin and smooth the top. Cover and freeze for 8 hours.

Coulis: take a small heavy saucepan, and over medium high heat, bring cherries, sugar, water and lemon juice to a boil. Simmer for eight minutes, or until the fruit breaks down a little.

Cool slightly and puree the mixture in a blender or processor, then pour through a sieve, pressing on solids to release juices. Chill in the fridge.

To serve, turn out onto a serving plate. Run a knife under hot water and slice, rinsing the knife after each cut. Place a slice on each plate, top with some cherry coulis and some extra chopped nougat as desired.

CHOCOLATE AND LOVE

Chocolate and Love was founded by Richard O'Connor and Birgitte Hovmand out of a love for superior chocolate, and a firm belief that good chocolate enjoyed in moderation should be a part of everyone's life. With the decision to convert to a majority organic diet after the birth of their daughter, Sophia, they struggled to find quality organic chocolate so decided to make their own. Chocolate and Love was born. They have a range of seven distinct bars each a blend of high quality cacao and all natural ingredients, and certified organic. These fair trade chocolate bars are made with cacao beans chosen for their fantastic flavour profile, from San Martin in the central Amazonian area, and the Apurimac Valley in Peru, the Yamasa area in The Dominican Republic and the Talamanca mountain range in Panama. Chocolate and Love also believe in giving something back and through a reforestation programme, weforest.org, have planted 22,000 trees to date. The firm has won a gold or silver taste award for every flavour and most recently picked up 5 Great Taste 2015 awards.

www.therarebrandmarket.co.uk/ chocolateandlove

CHOCOLATE AND LOVE PANAMA 80% CHOCOLATE

PREP: UNDER 15 MINS   **SERVES:** MANY

COOK: UNDER 15 MINS

INGREDIENTS

1 bar Chocolate and Love Panama
80% Chocolate, broken into pieces
½ tbsp agave nectar
1 punnet of fresh raspberries
1 tbsp coconut oil

METHOD

In a small pan on a low heat, melt the chocolate and add agave nectar and coconut oil.

Spoon the chocolate mixture into a pastry bag with a small nozzle. Line a baking tray with parchment, arrange raspberries and fill each with chocolate. Chill in the fridge until time to serve.

SILVER LANTERN TEA

Silver Lantern Tea provides high quality loose-leaf black, green and white teas from the familiar Jasmine and Ceylon, to lesser known Gunpowder and Keemun. Their tisanes (not technically a tea as they are not made from a tea bush), can be enjoyed on their own or customised to your own personal taste through blending at home.

Several of Silver Lanterns teas were winners of 2015 Great Taste awards and were sourced because of their taste and large leaf appearance. There is nothing quite like watching those beautifully big tea leaves unfurl as the hot water envelops them to bring a mindful moment to your day. The company website is full of tips to enhance your tea making experience: blending, brewing and advice on which tea suits the occasion.

www.therarebrandmarket.co.uk/ silverlanterntea

SMOKED LAYER CAKE

SILVER LANTERN TEA KEEMUN TEA

PREP: UNDER 1 HR   **SERVES:** 10

COOK: 2 HRS   **PRE HEAT OVEN:** 175C

INGREDIENTS

Chocolate base:
155g dark chocolate, broken
115g unsalted butter
150g golden caster sugar
55g light brown muscovado sugar
80g plain organic flour
1 tbsp unsweetened cocoa powder
½ tsp salt, finely ground
3 large free range eggs
1tsp vanilla extract
80g walnuts, coarsely chopped

Sponge:
220g plain flour
¾ tsp baking powder
½ tsp bicarbonate of soda
150g unsalted butter
130g golden caster sugar
2 large organic eggs
1 vanilla pod
140g organic Greek yoghurt
1 large pear, peeled and finely diced
 180g walnuts - for topping
2 tsp Silver Lantern keemun Tea
2 tsp Silver Lantern Lapsang Souchong Tea
70 ml boiling water

Smoky caramel:
100ml double cream
2 tbsp Silver Lantern Keemun Tea
2 tbsp Silver Lantern Lapsang Souchong Tea
4 tbsp cold water
115g golden caster sugar
115g unsalted butter

METHOD

Grease a 20 cm square brownie tin with melted butter and line with baking parchment.

Place 2 teaspoons each of the keemun and lapsang souchong tea in a bowl with 70 ml boiling water and leave to infuse.

Chocolate Base: Melt the chocolate and butter in a large heatproof bowl over simmering water. Turn off heat and whisk in both types of sugar. Leave to cool. Sieve the flour, cocoa and salt together. Break the eggs into a jug with the vanilla extract and beat together, then gently whisk fully into the chocolate mixture, finally fold in the flour. Stir in the chopped walnuts. Spread the mixture evenly in the tin and place in the middle of the oven. Bake for 20 minutes.

In a small pan bring the cream, for the caramel, just to the boil then remove from the heat. Add the remaining tea mix leaves, stir and leave to infuse, for about 20 mins then strain.

Sponge layer: use the same cake tin as you did previously, oven temperature remains the same. Using a mixer, cream the butter and sugar.

Beat the eggs in a jug with the vanilla pod seeds. Gradually add to the butter and sugar, beating constantly.

Add bicarbonate of soda and baking powder to flour. Slowly add to mixer and beat, followed by the yogurt. Then fold in the pear and the infused, strained tea water.

Pour into tin. Bake in the centre of the pre-heated oven for approximately 35 minutes, until cooked. Place on a wire rack to cool.

Smokey Caramel: re-heat the infused cream until nearly boiling. Put the four tbsp of water into a pan, add the caster sugar. Stir over low heat to dissolve, then turn up the heat to medium and leave, without stirring, to caramelise to a dark, nutty amber colour. Stir in the infused cream; it will hiss and bubble up but continue stirring, until calm whilst gradually adding the butter, leave to cool and thicken.

Assemble: Lay out the chocolate base, spread with a little of the smoky caramel. Place the sponge cake on top then gently spread more smoky caramel mixed with the chopped walnuts.

Pocket Feasts and Cake...

IN THIS SECTION YOU WILL FIND TEN CLEVER RECIPES FOR THE KIND OF FOOD THAT FITS IN YOUR POCKET, INCLUDING THE ALL IMPORTANT CAKE!

Elderflower

SPOON CEREALS

Spoon Cereals was founded by muesli and granola addicts, Annie Morris and Jonny Shimmin, after they had struggled to find a breakfast cereal to set them up for a day at the office. Spoon Cereals are a London-based premium, handmade granola brand. The aim of the business is to keep things simple: make perfect pots of wholesome granola using high-quality, all-natural ingredients - and most importantly no sugar, just maple syrup.

In 2013 the business was launched at a small food fair in London, serving their signature homemade granola pots. After six months of successful trading the pair pitched their business on the BBC's, Dragons' Den. They successfully secured investment from both Peter Jones and Deborah Meaden, who with their own experience in the food industry, have helped Annie and Jonny work towards their business goals. Spoon Cereals have branched out from the classic Granola and Muesli to a cinnamon and pecan mix, as well as a peanut and apple mix, to make even more brilliant breakfasts.

www.therarebrandmarket.co.uk/spooncereals

SPOON CEREALS PECAN AND CINNAMON GRANOLA

PREP: UNDER 15 MINS   **SERVES:** 12

COOK: UNDER 30 MINS   **PRE HEAT OVEN:** 160C

INGREDIENTS

225g almond butter
2 bananas, mashed
80g whole almonds
60g dried apricots
60g dried cherries
60g raisins
1-2 tbsp honey

40g mixed seeds ... whatever you have to hand
100g Spoon Cereals Pecan and Cinnamon Granola

METHOD

Line a baking tray with parchment paper.

In a small pan, heat the almond butter and mashed bananas. Stir gently until the mixture is soft and well combined. Set aside.

In a food processor, coarse chop the almonds, apricots, raisins and cherries. Transfer to a bowl. Mix in the seeds, honey and granola. Finally fold in the almond butter mixture. Press into prepared baking tray. Bake for 20-25 minutes until browned. Let it cool before cutting out into bars.

These will keep well in a sealed container for up to 2 weeks and are a perfect snack on the move for grown ups and kids alike.

DOISY & DAM

Doisy & Dam is co-founded by best friends Edward Smith & Richard Wilkinson. They named the brand after Nobel prize-winning scientists for their work in the field of health and nutrition, in the 1940's.

The friends are on a mission to bring a bit of well-deserved healthy indulgence into our lives. Each 'superdelicious' chocolate bar is lovingly hand-crafted in the UK using the best quality, organic ingredients, ethically sourced from all over the world. Their organic chocolate is gluten-free, soya-free and made up of cocoa mass, cocoa butter, sugar and a touch of vanilla powder. Next comes the health kick - it is enhanced by incredible superfoods such as maca, hemp, spirulina and sprouted buckwheat. Each bar is transformed into a wonderfully indulgent treat with a unique taste and texture. D&D like to keep it simple - there are no hidden ingredients and nothing artificial, just 'superdelicious', real food.
www.therarebrandmarket.co.uk/doisyanddam

DOISY &DAM
superdeliciousfood

LUCUMA LAMINGTONS

DOISY & DAM COCONUT AND LUCUMA 74% ORGANIC DARK CHOCOLATE

PREP: **UNDER 30 MINS** SERVES: **8-10**

COOK: **UNDER 1 HR** PRE HEAT OVEN: **170C**

INGREDIENTS

300g golden caster sugar
50g cocoa
75ml milk
50g unsalted butter
50g Doisy & Dam
Coconut and Lucuma
Dark Chocolate
50ml sunflower oil
4 medium eggs
100ml low-fat natural
yoghurt
3 tsp vanilla extract
175g plain flour

3 tsp baking powder

Coating:
15g cocoa
50ml cold milk
175ml boiling water
200g Doisy & Dam
Coconut and Lucuma
Dark Chocolate, finely
chopped
450g icing sugar
500g coconut desiccated

METHOD

Line a deep, 20cm square cake tin with baking parchment.

Put the sugar and cocoa in a bowl and beat in the milk. Melt the butter and chocolate in a saucepan and add to the sugar mix. Pour in the oil, add the eggs and beat until smooth. Stir in the yoghurt and vanilla, and mix in the flour and baking powder.

Pour the mix into the tin, cover with foil and bake for 45 mins, taking off the foil for the last 15 minutes. Remove from the oven, leave to cool in the tin and then cover with cling film.

For the coating, mix the cocoa and milk until smooth, whisk in the boiling water, stir in the chocolate until melted. Whisk in the icing sugar until dissolved and pour into a wide bowl. Put the desiccated coconut on a plate. Cut the cake into nine pieces and dunk each piece in the coating and fish out with two forks. Roll in coconut and leave to set on a wire tray. Repeat with remaining cake, icing and coconut.

HILLSIDE FOODS

Since Hillside was founded by former chef, Jay Allan in 2008, they have been dedicated to creating the ultimate cheeseboard accompaniments. Their multi award-winning range comprises savoury biscuits, fruit cheeses, pickles and chutneys. Located in Devon, the kitchens are a place where creativity, tradition and the finest ingredients come together to create unique recipes. They continue to win coveted food industry awards every year. Most recently, their Lemon Curd for Selfridges scooped a 3-Star Gold and Top 50 Foods in Britain, at the Great Taste awards 2015. Other award winners that year were their Celery Pickle, and Plum and Port Fruit for Cheese, plus a further four for their cheese biscuits with original flavours such as Pink Peppercorn, Charcoal and Cumin.

www.therarebrandmarket.co.uk/hillsidefoods

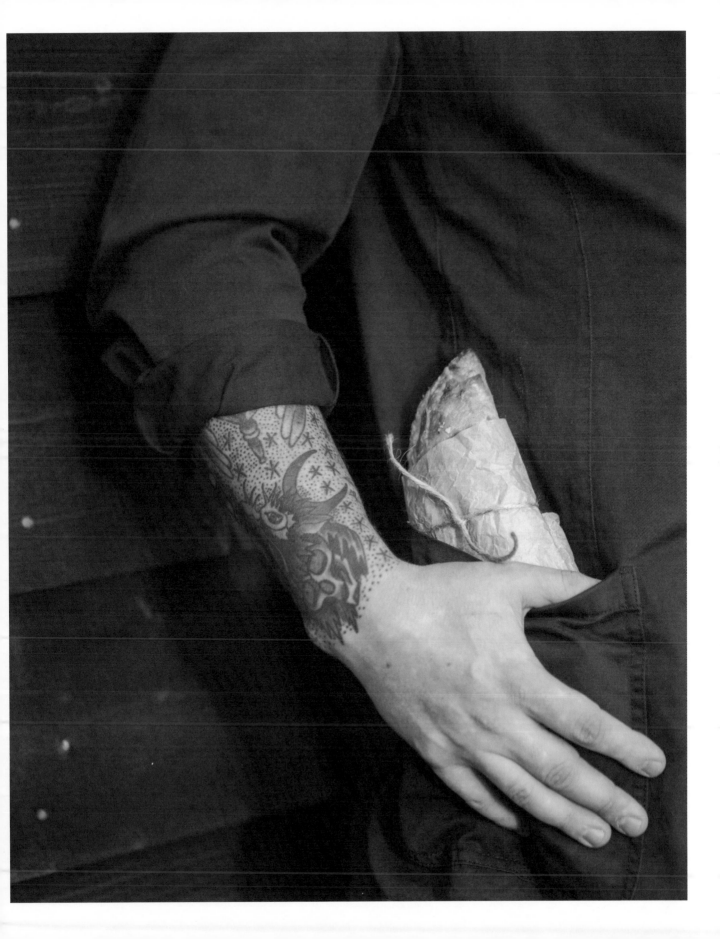

HILLSIDE FOODS PLUM AND PORT CHUTNEY

PREP: UNDER 15 MINS   **SERVES:** 2

COOK: UNDER 30 MINS   **PRE HEAT OVEN:** 180C

INGREDIENTS

Pack of shortcrust pastry
1 leek, sliced
knob of butter
200g smoked ham
handful flat leaf parsley, roughly chopped
70g Hillside Foods Plum and Port Chutney
1 free range egg, beaten

METHOD

For a fantastic lunch on the move or a tasty addition to a summer's picnic.

In a frying pan saute the leeks in butter until they are soft and shiny. Add the ham, flat leaf parsley and chutney. Combine the mixture together gently and thoroughly.

Roll out the pastry and, using a 20cm lid or bowl, cut out two circles.

Line a baking tray with parchment and lay out pastry circles. Spoon the filling, just off centre following the pastry curve. Brush the edge of the pastry with the egg.

Fold over and pinch to close, using the pasty print; practise makes perfect. Glaze with beaten egg and bake for 15 minutes or until the pastry is golden brown.

DONHEAD APPLE COMPANY

The philosophy of making a good cider is the combination of the best quality cider apples and a great deal of patience. So say Gavin and Kevin, who tend their orchard of traditional cider apple varieties in the beautiful village of Donhead St Mary tucked away on the border between Dorset and Wiltshire.

Not all apples are created equally - at Donhead, they know the the best cider is made from late season varieties such as Kingston Black, Dabinette and Yarlington Mill. Cider apples tend to be smaller, less juicy and mouth-puckeringly high in tannin. Not much fun to eat, but perfect for pressing at the peak of their ripeness and fermenting slowly, over the winter months. The freshly pressed cider juices are then left to slowly ferment and mature for several more months, to allow the flavour to develop and the tannins to soften. The cider is gently carbonated before bottling to give the mouthfeel of a fine mousse - which might sound a tad unusual but goes down well when drunk by locals, and judges of the 2015 Great Taste awards alike.

www.therarebrandmarket.co.uk/donheadapple

CLASSIC BRITISH CIDER APPLE JELLY

DONHEAD CRAFT CIDER

PREP: UNDER 30 MINS   **SERVES:** MAKES 1 LITRE KILNER JAR

COOK: 15 MINS

INGREDIENTS

600 ml Donhead Craft Cider
2 sticks cinnamon
1 tsp ground cloves
knob of fresh ginger
10g pectin
140g jam sugar

METHOD

In a large pan, add the cider, cloves, cinnamon and ginger. Warm through to let the flavours infuse.

Strain the liquid putting the cider back in the pan with the pectin and the sugar.

Bring to the boil. Remove from the heat. Strain into the sterile jar. Leave to cool. It is a great addition to any cheeseboard or meat pie.

ASKADA

Evaggelia Mytala's love for figs led her to the magical place of Kymi, on the island of Evia in Greece. On the organic fig farm, she wanted to preserve the authentic Mediterranean flavours which represented her childhood memories, and to recreate the same "askada" as "Grandma Sofia" and "Aunt Katina".

She believes that in this particular place, she has found the trees that bear these special fruits, with their delicate skin and remarkable taste. As well as the incomparable environment, the drying of the figs requires attention. Following tradition, the figs are carefully collected by hand around the end of August. The fruit is cut to bring the inside out and, once opened up, they take a rest sunbathing and absorbing all the rays of the Mediterranean light. Each and every fig is personally handled with enough care and love to make Grandma Sofia proud.

www.therarebrandmarket.co.uk/askada

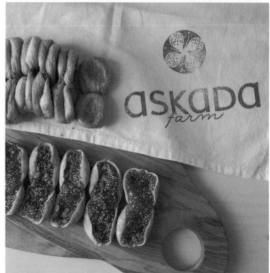

ASKADA FARM SUN DRIED KYMI FIGS

PREP: UNDER 15 MINS   **SERVES:** 2-4

COOK: UNDER 30 MINS   **PRE HEAT OVEN:** 205C

INGREDIENTS

500g wholewheat pizza dough (try the Pizza Dough Company)

200g Askada Farm Dried Kymi Figs - keep some back for decoration

1 large handful of wild rocket

1 tub of roasted tomato, garlic or plain houmous

1 medium onion, diced

200g hard cheese, grated

60g cherry tomatoes, sliced

60ml argan oil

3 tbsp fresh sage, chopped

balsamic vinegar for drizzling

sea salt

METHOD

Roll out pizza dough into a rectangle. Bake for 6-8 minutes and place on a wire cooling rack.

In large saucepan, heat the oil and then add onions, figs, sage and salt. Cook until figs are softened, approximately 3-4 minutes on medium heat. Remove from heat.

Paint the edges of pizza base with oil and then spread the houmous, followed by half the cheese and then the fig relish on the top. Evenly top with tomatoes, rocket and any remaining figs.

Sprinkle remaining cheese on top.

Bake pizza for 8-10 minutes or until desired crust is achieved and dough is fully cooked. Drizzle pizza with balsamic vinegar. Slice into squares.

BELINDA CLARK GOURMET CONFECTIONER

The fact that Belinda Clark's mother was a terrible cook, originally inspired Belinda to fall in love with cooking. Born with a sweet tooth and taking pride and joy in every dish she made it was a natural step into artisan confectionary. "When I made and tasted my first gourmet marshmallow, I knew that somehow my life had changed" says Clark. "It was like nothing I had ever tasted! And, when I shared my delicious treats with my friends they all loved it too." From then on it was her mission to inspire more people to eat delicious artisan confectionery. She wanted to create sweets that grown-ups would want to eat and share - to alter their expectations of sweets.

"I know it sounds cheesy, but my life has been transformed by gourmet confectionery," she adds. "I'm not afraid to say there is nothing else like my products out there, because there really isn't and I want to share that with others."

www.therarebrandmarket.co.uk/belindaclark

TORCHED MALLOW CAKE

BELINDA CLARK RASPBERRY MARSHMALLOWS

PREP: UNDER 30 MINS   **SERVES:** 8-10

COOK: UNDER 45 MINS   **PRE HEAT OVEN:** 180C

INGREDIENTS

25g butter, softened
200g golden castor
sugar
3 eggs
½ tsp lemon zest
200g self-raising flour
200g natural yoghurt

Topping:
80ml water

150g golden caster
sugar
1 tbsp lemon juice
1 tbsp elderflower
cordial (concentrate)
150g raspberries
3 pkts Belinda
Clark Raspberry
Marshmallows

METHOD

Grease a 25cm flan case and line with baking paper.

Beat the butter and sugar together until pale and fluffy. Beat in the eggs, one at a time. Gently fold in the lemon zest and flour and then fold in the yoghurt. Pour the mix into flan case.

Bake for 15-20 minutes or until a skewer comes out clean. When the cake is cooked, remove it from the oven, but leave it in the tin. Prick a fine skewer all over the surface of the cake.

Heat the water, sugar and lemon juice in a small saucepan and simmer for five minutes.

Remove the syrup from the heat and add the elderflower cordial, then spoon the syrup slowly over the top of the cake so it soaks into the holes rather than running to the edges. Dot the cake with the marshmallows and some fresh raspberries and either put it under the grill, until they are slightly browned or, if you have one, gently blowtorch the marshmallows.

PRIMROSE HILL TEAS

Primrose Hill Teas are an independent family run business based in London. They believe a harmonious blend of quality and healthy ingredients, and a balanced lifestyle is the key to feeling great. Their idea is a simple: use the highest quality tea leaves and ingredients in the creation of blends that boost natural health, while enjoying exceptional flavours. At the Great Taste awards 2015 they won 4 awards for their blends. Two stars for their White Jasmine Neroli and their Milk Oolong. The former is an exquisite Jasmine Silver Needle tea, blended with honey sweet orange blossoms. This white tea contains only the youngest buds of the tea bush, and is scented by carefully layering the tea with fresh Jasmine blossoms overnight and then painstakingly, removing the Jasmine once the aroma has been absorbed. This process is repeated up to seven times. The Oolong blend is delicate and produced when the leaf provides the creamiest character, naturally; reputed to boost metabolism, the taste is simply exquisite.

www.therarebrandmarket.co.uk/ primrosehillteas

PRIMROSE HILL TEAS JASMINE TEA

PREP: UNDER 1 HOUR   **SERVES:** 8

COOK: UNDER 1 HOUR   **PRE HEAT OVEN:** 180C

INGREDIENTS

160g golden caster sugar
150ml vegetable oil
1 tsp vanilla essence
250g plain flour
½ bicarbonate soda
½ tsp salt
2 free range eggs
200ml plain yogurt
4 tsp Primrose Hill Tea Jasmine Tea

For the lemon cream:
4 tsp Primrose Hill Tea Jasmine Tea left to soak, finely chopped
250ml of whipping cream
1 tbsp icing sugar
2 lemons, juice and zest

METHOD

Grease a large non-stick loaf tin very thoroughly. Place 4 tsp jasmine tea in a small amount of warm water to soften.

Whisk the oil, sugar, egg, yogurt and vanilla in a large bowl for about 5 mins, before adding the Jasmine Tea, flour, bicarbonate of soda and salt. Keep mixing until combined. Pour the mixture into loaf tin and bake for 40-45 mins until golden brown.

Using a skewer check the cake is ready - a clean skewer means it is done. Leave to cool fully before turning out onto a wire rack.

Whip the cream and icing sugar until stiff and then fold in the soaked jasmine tea until well mixed. Add the lemon juice and zest, mix again. When the cake is cool, smooth the cream on top of the loaf and serve.

PLAN BEE

More of a movement than just a business, Plan Bee are out to change the world one beehive at a time. They work with partnership businesses across the country to help protect and preserve dwindling honeybee numbers. Founder, Warren Bader was a film and music video producer working with the likes of Ridley Scott, Tina Turner and Michael Jackson. In order to get away from the stresses of the industry he rented an allotment and started growing heritage fruit trees; to help pollinate the trees he acquired some bees and the rest is history.

Plan Bee is the company behind the premium Origin Honey and Beehive Brae brands. Origin sources honey from the company's sustainably managed beehives across Scotland, working in hive management partnerships with some of the biggest and most environmentally-minded businesses in the country. Origin's artisan honey brand has a total of three Great Taste awards' gold stars to their name. Its stablemate Beehive Brae Mead also found success at the awards, with the innovative Elderflower and Rose Mead delivering a high quality product into a growing niche market.

Plan Bee delights in helping individuals, schools and companies improve their bee knowledge and up their green credentials, through their fully managed beehive service.

www.therarebrandmarket.co.uk/planbeeltd

BEE HIVE BRAE HONEY MEAD

PREP: UNDER 1 HOUR   **SERVES:** 8

COOK: UNDER 1.5 HOURS   **PRE HEAT OVEN:** 160C

INGREDIENTS

1 x 26 cm bundt pan or square 20cm cake tin
450g plain flour
¾ tsp baking powder
¾ tsp bicarbonate of soda
190g soft unsalted butter
4 oranges, 2 finely sliced, 1 juiced, 1 zest
250g granulated sugar
3 free range eggs
250ml buttermilk
250g golden caster sugar
non-stick cooking spray (or vegetable oil and
all-purpose flour, for greasing)
1 Bottle Beehive Brae Mead
handful of almonds, roughly chopped

Almond Mead Cream:
250ml chilled whipping cream
1 orange zest
100g whole almonds roasted and chopped
1 ½ tbsp golden caster sugar
25 ml Beehive Brae Mead honey

METHOD

Almond Mead Cream: Lightly whip the cream into soft peaks and mix in the orange zest, sugar, 75g of chopped almonds and 25ml honey mead. Cover and place in the fridge.

Place the finely sliced oranges and 150ml of mead in a saucepan and simmer for five minutes, until the oranges are cooked. Remove the oranges - but keep the oranges to line the cake tin and the mead for the glaze.

Spray the inside of the bundt pan with non-stick cooking spray. Or, mix together two teaspoons of flour and oil and brush all over the inside making sure you get into the crevices of the pan.

Line the bottom of the pan with slightly overlapping orange slices.

Sift the flour, baking powder, and bicarbonate of soda in a bowl.

In a mixer bowl, add the butter and zest of both oranges and beat until smooth creamy. Then add the sugar and beat again.

Add the eggs with a spoonful of the flour and mix. Then add the remaining flour and, when the mixture is smooth, slowly add the buttermilk until it is all blended together.

Finally gently mix the juice of one orange and 50ml of the mead into the mixture. Pour into the prepared bundt pan.

Place in the oven on a baking tray and bake for approximately 1¼ hours. Check after 60 minutes to see if it is cooked. When a skewer comes out clean, remove the cake to a wire rack and leave in its pan for 15 minutes before carefully turning out.

Leave the cake to cool, on a wire rack over a tray to catch the dribbles from the glaze. Add two tablespoons of sugar to the remaining mead in the saucepan and simmer reducing by 1/3 to create a glaze. When it has cooled pour all over the cake and sprinkle with the remaining chopped almonds and serve with the chilled almond cream.

AKESSON

Located in the Sambirano Valley, in the North-West of Madagascar, Bertil Åkesson's estate spreads over about 2000 hectares. Since 1920, the Åkesson estates have produced world-famous aromatic cocoa. Nearly one hundred years later most of the top chefs and chocolate makers around the world use the cocoa from these estates. Working closely with these inspiring people, Åkesson wanted to give his own interpretation of chocolate, and as a planter wanted to bring out the true taste of cocoa behind chocolate. So in 2009, he launched his own brand. He is now the winner of several culinary awards including a gold Great Taste award for his single estate chocolate Ambolikapiky Plantation.

www.therarebrandmarket.co.uk/ akessonsorganic

MASCARPONE AND COCOA COOKIES

AKESSON'S BRAZIL FORASTERO 75% DARK CHOCOLATE, COFFEE AND NIBS BAR

PREP: **35 MINS**   MAKES: **4 DOZEN**

COOK: **20 MINS**   PRE HEAT OVEN: **175C**

INGREDIENTS

480g plain flour
1 1/4 tsp coarse salt
250g unsalted butter, soft
180g mascarpone
250g golden caster sugar
2 tbsp pure vanilla extract
180g Akesson's Brazil Coffee Nib and Dark
Chocolate

METHOD

Mix flour and salt in a large bowl, set aside. In the bowl of an electric mixer, place the butter and mascarpone. Beat on medium speed until pale and fluffy. Add sugar and vanilla.

While mixer is running on low-speed, add flour mixture, until combined and then add the chocolate nibs.

Divide the dough into half, shape into two logs about 8cm wide and wrap each one in parchment paper. Freeze for a minimum of 30 minutes. Alternatively you can keep these in the freezer for up to two weeks before baking.

Lightly flour a cool surface. Unwrap one log and roll out, keeping it quite thick. Use a 4cm cutter to cut out cookies, and place on a baking sheet lined with baking parchment spacing them well apart. Bake until golden around edges, 12 -16 minutes. Let the cookies cool slightly before moving to a wire rack to cool completely.

CANESMITH & CO

Canesmith & Co make gourmet sweets for grown ups. All the confectionery is crafted using the best possible ingredients, and takes inspiration from modern food trends and childhood favourites. They make a wide range of delicious treats: from chewy caramels and salt water taffies, to tangy sherbet and real fruit lollipops. Canesmith are taking sweets in a new direction. They are creating modern candy and bringing sweets up to date positioning them as accomplished premium products similar to chocolate, ice cream and popcorn. A key success for the brand was being chosen by Selfridges as part of their Meet the Makers campaign. Canesmith & Co is doing something different in sugar confectionery, and this was recognised by the food community when they won 5 Great Taste awards for their products in 2015. This truly demonstrates that 'gourmet sweets' work as a concept.

www.therarebrandmarket.co.uk/canesmith

CANESMITH SOY AND SESAME CARAMEL

PREP: 1 HOUR   **SERVES:** 12-16

COOK: 1 HOUR

INGREDIENTS

Sunflower oil - the amount depends on your deep fat fryer
Dough:
500g strong white flour
50g caster sugar
40g unsalted butter
2 free-range eggs
2 x 7g sachets instant yeast

10g salt
150ml warm milk
130ml water

Coating:
2 x pkts Canesmith Soy and Sesame Caramels
100ml double cream
2 tbsp sesame seeds

METHOD

You will need a deep-fat fryer to make doughnuts. Put 100ml water and all other dough ingredients into a large bowl. Stir with your hands until a dough is formed. Slowly add the remaining water and knead the dough in the bowl for four minutes. Or if you have electric mixer you could use the dough hook attachment.

Tip dough onto a lightly floured surface and knead for ten minutes until the dough is smooth and elastic. Place in a clean bowl, cover with a damp tea towel, leave to rise. After an hour tip the dough out onto a very lightly floured surface and knock it back by kneading it a few times. Divide the dough into 10 equal portions and shape each portion into a ball and leave to rise for an hour.

Preheat a deep fat fryer, filled with sunflower oil, to 180C. Lower each doughnut into the fryer, cooking each side for about five minutes or until golden brown. Remove the doughnuts from the oil with a slotted spoon and immediately roll in caster sugar. Set aside and leave to cool.

Place the caramels and cream in a saucepan on a low heat, until the caramels have melted. Remove from the heat. When cool pour the glaze over the doughnuts and sprinkle with sesame seeds.

Food Stories Brand Watch...

FOR THIS SECTION FOOD STORIES ASKED SOME OF THE UK'S MOST TALENTED WRITERS TO REVIEW EMERGING RARE ALCOHOL BRANDS, LUCKY THEM!

ALSO BROWSE THE EDITOR'S PICKS FOR BRANDS TO WATCH.

ILLUSTRATIONS SUPPLIED BY WWW.SIVELLINK.DK

BEER AND ALE CHARTER

Written by Pete Brown

When people look for the cause of a revolution, they tend to make the mistake of thinking there'll be one simple answer. But when I studied history at school, I learned the seven different causes of the French revolution - separate strands that combined at the right time in the right fashion to create a seismic event.

It's not unreasonable to call the surge of interest in beer a revolution, it's transforming the way we drink and think about beer and is sure to wreak a permanent change on our drinking habits. And like any good revolution, it has various causes.

The boom in British brewing dates back to 2002, when Gordon Brown introduced tax breaks for microbrewers that allowed them to compete with the big boys. After decades of decline, the number of brewers in Britain surged upwards. But that didn't make for a revolution on its own. For the first few years, all these new brewers were creating very similar beers: a typical British brown ale or bitter, somewhere between 3.6% and 4.2% ABV, and maybe a golden ale, slightly lighter and fresher.

And then, the world shrank.

Britain has one of the world's great brewing traditions. We might not realise it, but our real ale is admired and copied by brewers the world over. It's one of three or four great European beacons of beery excellence, alongside the pilsners of the Czech Republic, the variety of lagers found across Germany, and the sheer, wonderful craziness of Belgian brewing. Until a decade ago, each of these revered styles sat respectfully within its own tradition. Britain brewed ale, Germany and the Czech Republic brewed lager, and the Belgians brewed strong abbey beers, wild, spontaneously fermented beers, spicy saisons, and anything else they could think of. (I once had a Belgian mustard beer. Reader, I finished my glass.)

American craft brewers, with no real tradition of their own, looked to these four and began to copy them and, eventually, mastered them. And then social media happened - a second driver of revolution. The world's brewing community - bloggers, drinkers, importers, pubs and brewers themselves - began a permanent, ongoing conversation about beer styles and ideas, and the walls came down. Those different traditions are now merging and cross-pollinating. Beer is starting to lose its national identity, and craft beer is becoming a global whole that is greater than the sum of its parts.

The new world of brewing sees Belgian-style wild yeasts entering British ales, traditional British dry-hopping being applied to Czech-style pilsners, and herbs and spices that haven't been seen in beer for centuries making an epic return.

So here are five beers brewed by British breweries (the eldest of whom is only eleven years old this year) combining different brewing traditions, and pushing beer far beyond its conventional ingredients list to achieve stunning results.

01|09 Hibiscus & Chamomile Saison (5.6% ABV)

Brew By Numbers, London say: "We add hops to beer because over the centuries, they've proven to have preservative properties as well as bags of flavour. But before hops came along we flavoured beer with anything from the hedgerow or field." Here's a wonderful take on the Belgian saison tradition that's kept this idea alive.

www.brewbynumbers.com

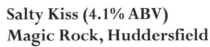

BREW BY NUMBERS

— BBNº —

Salty Kiss (4.1% ABV)
Magic Rock, Huddersfield

Based on the increasingly rare German Göse style, this beer brewed with added salt is nowhere near as bad as it sounds. Think seltzer-like refreshment rather than seawater, and you start to understand what an intriguing idea this is.

www.magicrockbrewing.com

Redwood (5.8% ABV)
Wild Beer Co, Somerset

When Wild Beer Co launched in 2012 their manifesto was to always add a fifth ingredient to the traditional four that make beer, usually something foraged from near the brewery. Redwood is the culmination of their art, with locally foraged fruits, Belgian-inspired wild yeasts and beer aged in barrels for a year before being carefully blended with previous vintages.

www.wildbeerco.com

THE WILD BEER CO

Otto (8% ABV)
Thornbridge, Bakewell, Derbyshire

Head Brewer Rob Lovatt is inspired by the unsung variety of brewing traditions in Germany and is wonderfully adept at accurately recreating them. Otto is a Weizen doppelbock, brewed with wheat as well as the normal barley, and shows off deep aromas of bubblegum, banana and cloves, with a hint of toffee.

Thornbridge
BREWERY

www.thornbridgebrewery.co.uk

KNACKERED MOTHER'S WINE CLUB EDIT

Written by Helen McGinn

IF I HAD TO CHOOSE A DESERT ISLAND DISH, IT WOULD BE ROAST CHICKEN. EVERY TIME. BUT UNTIL I'M ON THAT ISLAND, I WOULDN'T WANT TO EAT IT EVERY DAY. RATHER, I WANT A MIX OF SPICY, FRESH, CREAMY, SIMPLE AND DOWNRIGHT DECADENT DISHES - AND THAT'S JUST ONE WEEKEND'S WORTH. THE SAME GOES FOR WINE: I HAVE MY FAVOURITES BUT IT'S MORE A CASE OF SO MANY WINES, SO LITTLE TIME. WITH NEW SMALL SCALE PRODUCERS POPPING UP IN OLD WORLD COUNTRIES AND OLD PRODUCERS SETTING UP IN NEW COUNTRIES, THE WINE LANDSCAPE HAS NEVER LOOKED SO GOOD. HERE ARE A FEW SUGGESTIONS GUARANTEED TO SEND EVEN THE MOST WELL TRAVELLED TASTE BUDS OFF ON A TANGENT...

Wiston Estate

Nestled in the gentle slopes of the South Downs in Sussex lies a real hidden gem, Wiston Estate, where Harry & Pip Goring planted vines back in 2006. Thanks to a combination of ideal soils, climate (mostly!) and grape varieties, not to mention star winemaker Dermot Sugrue, they're now producing incredible sparkling wines that deserve to be taken as seriously as some of the best Champagnes. Their Rosé is a real treat.

WWW.WISTONESTATE.COM

WISTON
ESTATE
SOUTH DOWNS

Domaine Jones

For years Katie Jones worked in the wine industry here in the UK. One day she decided she wanted to make wine, not just sell it, so in 2008 she moved to the Languedoc in southern France and bought a vineyard. Since then she's gone on to buy two more small vineyards, winning a cabinet's worth of awards for her wine and marrying a fellow winemaker along the way. "A case of me and Monsieur Jones" as she so aptly puts it. If you love a big red, you'll fall for her Fitou.

WWW.DOMAINEJONES.COM

Vinteloper

Based in South Australia's Adelaide Hills region, winemaker David Bowley is very tall, very talented and rather partial to a tattoo. His wines are refreshingly different; seriously made but fun to drink. With their beautifully designed labels, they stand out for all the right reasons. My favourites include his Pinot Noir, Riesling and a Touriga Nacional. Told you it was refreshingly different.

WWW.VINTELOPER.COM.AU

Rossidi

For years, Bulgarian wine was more about quantity, rather than quality. But now, a new generation of winemakers is making Bulgaria one of the most exciting new-old-world countries to explore. At Rossidi, located in the Thracian Lowlands of Bulgaria, winemaker Edward Kourian believes it's all about planting the right grapes in the right places and letting Bulgaria's terroir do its thing. Cheers to that.

WWW.ROSSIDI.COM

Helen's book, The Knackered Mother's Wine Club, is out now (£7.99, Pan Macmillan). For weekly wine recommendations visit **WWW.KNACKEREDMOTHERSWINECLUB.COM**

COCKTAIL CHRONOLOGIES

Written by James Fowler

FOOD STORIES ASKED THE UK'S TOP MIXOLOGIST JAMES FOWLER TO CREATE SOME COCKTAILS USING RARE BRAND SPIRITS, CHAMPAGNE AND WINE WHILST TAKING INSPIRATION FROM SOME HISTORICAL COCKTAIL RECIPES.

1877

Gin Fizz
SEEDLIP

A non-alcoholic spirit; its flavour is packed with clove, citrus and a freshness of pine. Neat, it reminds me of Christmas. It is amazing with tonic and makes a great mock G & T. I've opted for a twist on the classic "Gin Fizz" similar to the well known "Tom Collins." The first printed reference to "fizz" is in the 1887 edition of Jerry Thomas Bartender's Guide, containing six such recipes. The fizz became widely popular in America between 1900 and the 1940s.

WWW.SEEDLIPDRINKS.COM

50ml Seedlip
10ml Lemon Verbena Gomme (Lemon Verbena Leaf brewed in sugar syrup)
20ml Red Grapefruit Juice
150ml Soda Water

Simply build all ingredients in a long glass filled with fresh cubed ices. Stir & serve.

1896

The Clover Club Cocktail
BRILLIANT GIN

Big bursts of botanicals - juniper, sage, coriander, angelica, savory, lemon peel, bitter orange, grains of paradise, cloves and cinnamon. It's beautifully smooth with a seaside mineral freshness.

Celebrating The Clover Club Cocktail, a drink that pre-dates Prohibition, and is named after the Philadelphia men's club which met in the Bellevue-Stratford Hotel until the 1920s.

WWW.BRILLIANTGIN.CO.UK

50ml Brilliant Gin
15ml Egg white
20ml fresh lemon juice
4 fresh raspberries

Get your cocktail shaker filled with fresh ice. Add all ingredients to shaker. Shake with passion until cold. Fine strain (use a tea stainer) into a cocktail coupe.

1919

The Negroni
KAMM & SONS

Kamm & Sons founder, Alex Kammerling, developed Kamm & Sons Ginsing Spirit, containing 45 botanicals, producing a spirit so unique it was the first British aperitif to be created since the early 1900s! I love it as a great option for Gin & Bitter lovers. Classically it screams one cocktail, "The Negroni," invented in 1919 in Florence where Count Negroni created "The Americano" cocktail.

WWW.KAMMANDSONS.COM

25ml Kamm & Sons
25ml Gin (Portobello road)
25ml Sweet Vermouth

Into a chosen short serving glass add fresh cubed ice. Add all ingredients & stir briefly. Serve with a wedge of orange.

1922

The Dirty Martini
CHILLGROVE VODKA

I've tried a few grape vodkas and this tops my list, it's the first grape vodka produced in the UK. It's clean, smooth and exciting with cocktails. I recently made a rather daring and dapper twist on a "Dirty Martini" using Chilgrove Vodka. The Martini is known as the only American invention as perfect as a 'sonnet' and by the roaring 20s was one of the most popular cocktails ever. Also a favourite with James Bond!

WWW.CHILLGROVESPIRITS.COM

45ml Perigord truffle infused vodka
10ml fresh goats cheese whey
Fresh lemon zest
Grated truffle

Fill mixing glass with fresh ice add all wet ingredients. Stir to chill & taste, dilute as necessary. Pour into a chilled Martini glass. Sprinkle grated truffle and lemon zest on top.

1934

The Skinny Bellini
SKINNY PROSECCO

Of the skinny range this is my favourite and has a really enjoyable palate, very well balanced and a great texture. Drier than most Proseccos but to me that's a special thing. Lets go to the classic Bellini with a sugar free puree. Creating what was to become known as the bellini cocktail in around 1934, Giuseppe Cipriani was inspired painter Giovanni Bellini and the pink glow portrayed in his many paintings.

WWW.THOMSONANDSCOTT.COM

25ml Sugar free pomegranate puree into a glass
Add 50ml of Prosecco
Stir to mix & foam
Top with 100ml of Prosecco.

Sweet Virtues is a health conscious lifestyle confectionary brand based on three values, to 'Nourish, Nuture, Grow.' Reflected in all their ingredients, which are sourced due to their nutrition values and superfood qualities, all the truffles are handmade in the UK, organic and dairy free they contain nothing artificial. Suitable for vegetarians and vegans and mouth-watering to eat. **www.sweetvirtues.co.uk**

BRANDS TO WATCH: 'FREE FROM'

Researched by www.nutrition-nutshell.com

IN EACH PUBLICATION OF FOOD STORIES WE FEATURE A SELECTION OF BRANDS THAT ARE WORTHY OF RECOGNITION WITHIN THE FOOD INDUSTRY. FOR OUR FIRST ADDITION WE HIGHLIGHT BRANDS INVOLVED IN SUPPLYING WONDERFUL 'FREE FROM' PRODUCTS...

Seedlip is the 'World's First Distilled Non-Alcoholic Spirit' based on herbal remedies published in the 'Art of Distillation' in 1651. Not only is it non-alcoholic but also sugar, sweetener and calorie free. Blended and bottled in the UK and full of botanicals sourced from around the world. Perfectly wonderful with ice and a slice. **www.seedlipdrinks.com**

Thomson & Scott Skinny are beautifully crafted no and low sugar Champagnes and Sparkling wines. "Super dry but beautifully balanced" Skinny champagne has 10-25 % less sugar than conventional champagne, with the line ever expanding. Never more so than now, can we celebrate pure enjoyment without the guilt. **www.thomsonandscott.com**

Plamil Foods based in Folkstone are the original vegan company in the UK. All their products are dairy, gluten and nut free; they are made using 100% renewable energy and are ethically sourced. Everyone, including those with most allergies or specific religious requirements, can enjoy all products that are on offer, safe in the knowledge that each product has been made with care, enjoyment and to the highest of standards.

www.plamilfoods.co.uk

Booja Booja are all about luxury yet with health at the fore-front. Rich and creamy ice cream, made with cashew nuts, other wholesome recipes full of organic ingredients and completely dairy, gluten and soya free. Pure enjoyment and mere delight from each and every spoonful. Exquisite and guilt-free recipes made with heart and soul.

www.boojabooja.com

Qnola are the first company to specialize in quinoa based breakfast products. They are nutritionally enhanced and developed without gluten, wheat, grains, dairy sugars or additives. The nourishing ingredients provide energizing and healing benefits, giving the body and mind the support it needs to be well and focused.

www.qnola.co.uk

Biofair are both fair trade and organic, all products are ethically sourced and are not only good for your health but support third world farmers too. They are committed to producing high quality organic foods to all. Their pasta is dairy, nut and gluten free. A perfect alternative, full of protein and simply delicious. Many different products for different dietary requirements.

www.biofair.co.uk

BRANDS TO WATCH: FABULOUS PLACES TO EAT AND SHOP

EACH ISSUE, FOOD STORIES FEATURES A SELECTION OF BRANDS THAT ARE WORTHY OF RECOGNITION WITHIN THE FOOD INDUSTRY - THIS ISSUE WE FOCUS ON INDEPENDENTS TO EAT WITH AND SHOP FROM! THERE IS NO BIAS TO LONDON OR A PARTICULAR PART OF THE UK AND IN FUTURE ISSUES WE MAY GO GOBAL!

Hill & Szrok Master Butcher & Cookshop based in East London, combine the best of tradition and modernity. By day they sell free range and organic meats from small English farms. As soon as the butchers closes their night jobs begin, cooking their food at their restaurant, serving up to 70 people per night. **www.hillandszrok.co.uk**

Upton Smokery and Farmshop based outside Burford in the heart of the Cotswolds not only smoke their own meat, fish and game on-site, but grow vegetables and make delicious food that can be sold in their wonderful farmshop, full of lots of local produce and other tempting delights. **www.uptonsmokery.co.uk**

Ed's Easy Diner is a much loved retro-American diner that first opened its doors in Soho over 25 years ago, and has now expanded to just under 50 locations. Unchanged and still true to the ethos "Quality Forever." Ed's is going strong and still full of fun, great food and a little bit of 'Rock and Roll.'

www.edseasydiner.com

Polo24hour Bar has been based outside Liverpool Street Station since 1953. "Food, drink and stories in comfort, no matter what the hour." Not only do they keep all Londoners happy within the confines of their restaurant, they also deliver to surrounding doorsteps and office desks.

www.polo24hourbar.co.uk

Situated in Midhurst, West Sussex, the farmshop represents the heart and holistic ethos of the Estate, much of their produce and meat is home grown and sourced to very high standard, the farm and butchery running along side each other to produce only the best. Attached is a café selling outstanding food from snacks to hearty meals.

www.cowdray.co.uk

Thank you Madeleine for supporting our first issue!

Madeleine Shaw, Health Ambassador for **Harrods**

www.madeleineshaw.com   **www.harrods.com**